A Friendly Human in Presales

A Friendly Human in Presales

How to Harness the Seven Timeless Behaviors to Drive Success in Technical Sales

Ron Whitson

A Friendly Human in Presales:
How to Harness the Seven Timeless Behaviors to Drive Success in Technical Sales

© Copyright 2024 Ron Whitson

All Rights Reserved. No part of this book may be reproduced, stored in a retrieval system, or transmitted in any form or by any means, electronic, mechanical, photocopying, recording, or otherwise, without the written prior permission of the author.

ISBN-13: 979-8-3294793-9-3
ISBN-10: 8329479393
ASIN: B0DDBYXCRG

www.TimelessBehaviors.com

Cover design by Owais Ashraf
Photograph by Ashley Carter
Icons designed by Jamie Pearson

Dedication

This book is dedicated to my dad, Ron Whitson Sr.
And my mother, Betty Ginn.

You instilled in me the belief that I can accomplish anything I choose to do. Your constant love, encouragement, and support are the greatest gifts anyone could receive from their parents.

Thank you, and I love you!

– Ron Whitson

What Readers Are Saying

The overwhelming theme of this book is to be yourself. I wish I had known that sooner in my own career. I applaud Ron for putting himself out there and bringing this collection of stories to the masses. We need more friendly humans in presales.

– Rew Dickinson
CEO, Alpha Presales

While it is absolutely important to work on your presentation skills, your discovery techniques, and your sales processes, Ron reminds us that the most important piece of the sales process is YOU, the Friendly Human! Working on yourself and how you relate to your customers is far more important than being the most technically knowledgeable person in the room.

– Jack Cochran
Presales Leader, Coach, and Podcast Producer

Reading this book feels like you're having a front porch conversation with Ron to understand why a friendly approach is a winning approach. In a season where it seems anyone with a camera and some charisma can be an "influencer" or "coach," Ron has reached deep into his personal experience to ground his readers in seven timeless truths. He has masterfully communicated how being a "friendly human" and a skilled seller co-exist and are co-requisites to a long and successful presales career. Recently, I've been increasingly asked by our clients at 2Win how they can ensure the persuasive skills we teach are used for good. A Friendly Human in Presales provides that answer in spades.

– Chad Wilson
Executive, Author, and Coach, 2Win! Global

As the General Manager of PreSales Collective, I've had the privilege of interviewing numerous presales professionals. A recurring theme in these conversations is the abundance of product training but a noticeable gap in structured soft-skills training. This is unfortunate because, as we know, the true art of presales lies in the nuanced realm of soft skills. Ron captures this perfectly in "A Friendly Human in Presales," where he outlines seven timeless behaviors that emphasize authenticity, empathy, storytelling, and more. Ron's genuine approach shines through in every page, making this a must-read for anyone looking to master the soft skills essential for success in presales—and in life."

– Chris Mabry
General Manager, PreSales Collective

Many of us who have had longevity in presales had to learn these "Timeless Behaviors" through trial and error—sometimes more trial and error than we'd like to remember. Ron's book nails the soft skills and behaviors that presales professionals must cultivate to truly connect with buyers and secure the technical win.

Ron's genuine passion for teaching these behaviors, coupled with his humility and humor, shines through every page. Packed with practical tips that you can implement immediately, this book is a must-read for anyone aiming to excel in presales. It stands as a timeless guide from someone who truly gets it. On top of that, he is the epitome of a "Friendly Human in Presales."

– Pam Dunn
SE Leader, Coach, Mentor, Strategic Advisor

A Friendly Human should be required reading for anyone in the Presales profession! Ron shares his vast experience, and more importantly, actionable exercises to help develop these Timeless Behaviors easily. After reading this book, I can confidently say the key to being a Friendly Human is being yourself!

– Asif Ahmad
Presales Leader, Solutions Consultant, and Tech Enthusiast

Having worked closely with Ron in various capacities—as a peer, direct report, and presales support—I can vouch for the insights and practical advice he shares in this book. Our time together was filled with learning and some occasional mischief, making the journey all the more memorable. During a team training session, we all used props to tell a convincing story. Some nearly fell out of their seats during the show-and-tell sessions, which only highlighted the effectiveness of these techniques. These experiences and the principles behind them are well-documented in Ron's book, providing a step-by-step guide to success in presales.

Ron's journey showcases the incredible transformation of a self-professed geek and nerd into a successful presales professional. He has learned from others, adapted those lessons to his style, and, in return, helped countless others on their path. His career is a testament to how perseverance and commitment can lead to excellence in presales.

I highly recommend "A Friendly Human in Presales" to anyone looking to excel in the presales field. You will find it both informative and engaging, filled with the practical wisdom that Ron has generously shared throughout his career.

– Chris Bangma
Presales Principal, Leader, Musician

You won't find a more genuinely friendly human in presales—or anywhere—than Ron Whitson. He lives and breathes the Seven Timeless Behaviors, not just as a presales leader but as a person. This isn't some manufactured list; it's a true reflection of who Ron is and how he connects with people. "A Friendly Human in Presales" offers an excellent roadmap for building meaningful connections, whether with prospects or colleagues and reminds us that no matter how technical we are, we all have the capacity to be friendly. Ron's conversational writing style and entertaining stories from the presales trenches make this book fun to read and provide invaluable tools for elevating your presales game. Enjoy!

– Don Martin
Presales Veteran, Coach, and Leader

Foreword by Shane Philips

Ron and I, along with a few others, have had the pleasure of navigating the world of presales for several decades. Nearly 30 years ago, I hired Ron into his first presales role, and since then, we've experienced numerous changes and developments together. We've presented during the shift from mainframe to client/server applications, from client/server to web-based applications, and now as we move toward container-based/cloud solutions. Technology is a fascinating field for building a career, but it comes with its challenges, especially when software companies fail to adequately prepare their sales teams.

This book is an invaluable resource for anyone in presales, tech sales, solutions consulting, or even traditional sales roles. It's not a book to read once and then shelve; rather, it's a guide to revisit continually. Each time you reference it, you'll uncover new insights and nuances about connecting with clients. In a landscape where sales opportunities are limited, you can't afford to lose a deal due to poor presentations, inadequate preparation, or overconfidence.

Ron naturally possesses some of the best instincts for connecting with clients, but what sets him apart is his relentless pursuit of improvement. He's never complacent; he dedicates significant time to refining his skills and mentoring others to do the same. In this book, Ron shares stories and invaluable lessons from his decades of meeting with prospects and customers. While the technology we work with has evolved dramatically, the core skills of building trust, understanding client needs, and effective communication have remained constant.

Throughout all these changes, one quality in Ron has always stood out: he is a friendly human. His approachability and genuine interest in others make him not just a great presales professional but also someone people want to work with and learn from. This friendly demeanor helps him build connections and establish trust, which are crucial elements in successful presales engagements.

The software business has become increasingly impatient, with results driving decisions. This impatience often leads to presales teams being inadequately prepared. They're expected to learn the software quickly and then present it. If a prospect can't distinguish your solution from competitors or see its value, you haven't done your job. Many leading software solutions are losing deals to new-generation software simply because of this lack of preparation.

Scripted demonstrations are NOT the answer.
One-size-fits-all demos are NOT the answer.
Your company's reputation alone is NOT the answer.

In this book, Ron breaks down how you, the presales engineer, can elevate your game and make a significant impact. You should not be the weak link in a sales cycle; instead, you should be the trusted advisor who, through your connection with clients, turns opportunities into purchases.

For any presales manager out there, advocating for more training on connecting with clients for your team is crucial. This book should be required reading for everyone on your team. Your success hinges on your team's performance, and if you're not actively helping them improve, chances are they won't.

– Shane Philips

Foreword by Brian Ivanovick

"It may sound overly simplistic, but we should all strive for sincerity in our thoughts, words, and actions."– Ron Whitson

Let me tell you a story about Ron Whitson. It's the story of how I hired Ron to be on our team at Percolate. It illustrates how he takes this "friendly human" thing very seriously.

When I first spoke with Ron, I was looking for someone to build out our Demo Engineering function. A recruiter connected us and set up an initial phone call. I was in our New York City office, and Ron was located just outside of Dallas. I explained to Ron what I was looking for. I wanted someone to come in, uplevel our demo environments, and make sure we could tell the best narratives with fresh, clean data. The phone went quiet for a few seconds longer than expected, and then Ron said something like: "Well, Brian, that's not exactly what I'm looking for. I'm really good at connecting with customers and telling stories about how software is going to help them achieve their goals. Are there any openings for someone like that on your team?". I was surprised by his candor, transparency, and clarity. Most people just don't come out and say something like that. They dance around it. Ron was different. He challenged my initial thinking, but I could tell, from his tone, that it was coming from a good place. It was like he was saying all of that with a smile on his face. You couldn't help but like the guy. And so I opened my mind to other possibilities. I thought to myself: Maybe I could use another person, provided they were good enough. And so we ended the conversation on good terms, and I took the afternoon to think about the next steps. I wanted to learn more. Maybe he could help us. So the next day, I introduced Ron to other colleagues and after a series of successful interviews, we ended up inviting him to do a final presentation at our office.

It was a crisp, sunny autumn day. There was that slight chill in the air, but the warmth of the recently departed summer lingered, provided you were walking on the sunny side of the sidewalk. Our office was located in Soho, amidst all of the best luxury and lifestyle brands of the day. For the traditionalists, you had brands like Apple, Coach and Prada. For the younger set, like our colleague "Swon", you had Supreme, Billionaire Boys Club, and Palace. I remember one day, the noise outside of our office was particularly loud. A boisterous group of young people had assembled, awaiting the hip-hop star Lil' Yachty's in-store visit. His arrival brought shouts and screams as his car was engulfed by the crowd on the cobblestone street below.

Our location made sense. Percolate was a marketing technology company helping brands better communicate with their customers and we were surrounded by some of the best brands with some of the best marketing in the world. We had a distinctive orange brand that could be seen in ads on taxis in New York City. Our founders were visionaries thinking about how brands were going to communicate with their customers over the next few decades. Percolate tended to attract employees who were on the same wavelength. The aforementioned "Swon" was a good example. He had his pulse on the most compelling brand stories of the day and didn't shy away from flashing off the latest clothing from brands like Kith, Palace, and Noah. This, dear reader, is the environment that Ron Whitson stepped into and landed himself his next Solution Consulting (SC) gig.

For those who don't know Ron, he's a warm-hearted, lifelong Texan, who will go out of his way to pick you up from the airport if you're visiting Dallas. When he does, it will be in an SUV, rocking some of the greatest hits of the 80s. He's not what I would call a Soho guy. So how the heck does this friendly human from Texas, with no experience selling marketing software, ingratiate himself into the world of the hip and want-to-be hip?

Ron arrived early that day, and I greeted him after getting a call from our recruiter. The first thing I noticed was that Ron was wearing a jacket with an orange pocket square and tie. He was on brand, something very important to an organization serving marketers. I led him into the interview room and gave him a few minutes to set up while I grabbed the rest of the panelists. When I returned, Ron had laid out orange binders for each of us with his updated resume inside. Each of these thoughtful details left an impression. Ron was a professional. He cared about making an impression.

Then it was time for the presentation. I expected to be bored to tears. Ron was selling software that monitored the performance of industrial equipment, and I thought that marketing software was inherently more interesting. As he started, Ron pulled us in. I remember him distinctly engaging each one of us to understand what we wanted to get out of the presentation. He made sure everyone's input was received. Unlike other candidates, he had a real conversation with people. He wanted to know about what they did and what they cared about. And none of this was phony. He genuinely cared to know what was important to you. Ron was quick to laugh and quick to make a little joke at his own expense. With each minute, he felt more friendly, approachable, and familiar. After developing some level of rapport with each of us, he proceeded with his presentation. In the back of my head, I remember thinking: I can't believe he wore an orange pocket square and tie and brought these orange binders in.

Then it was time for the demonstration. Remember Ron is presenting software that monitors industrial pumps to a bunch of New Yorkers immersed in brand marketing. But Ron was the consummate pro. He took us through the challenges that these companies face, and he underscored the implications of what happens when a pump fails. Each incident is a potential multi-million dollar problem. He helped us envision what happens when a pump fails. Crews of mechanics need to go out to the site to do the repairs. And each minute the pump is down, you're losing money. We felt the pain. It didn't matter that the interface looked like it was built in Windows 95, it helped companies avoid these calamities. And it was all so clear. We understood it, and we cared. We knew what was at stake and we knew that this was a potential solution. Most importantly we trusted the guy speaking with us because he took the time to show he cared about us.

After Ron left the room that day, all of these New Yorkers were sold. He joined the team about a month later and has been a dear friend ever since.

I'm excited for you to read this book. Creating a personal connection where buyers want to buy from you is one of the most durable competitive advantages you'll have. The behaviors described below are going to help you in your Presales career and your life. Buyers are exhausted from all of the industry jargon and buzzwords. They're exhausted from all of the salespeople blatantly acting solely in their self-interest. They're looking for friendly humans who care about them and whom they can trust. Ron Whitson lives his life this way and is the perfect guide to take you on this journey. Enjoy the ride!

– Brian Ivanovick

Preface

Welcome to "A Friendly Human in Presales: How to Harness the Seven Timeless Behaviors to Achieve Success in Technical Sales," and thank you for picking up my book. My name is Ron Whitson, and I have spent my career immersed in the dynamic world of presales, both as an individual contributor and a leader. Over the years, I've developed a deep passion for this profession and a commitment to helping others succeed.

Like many who venture into presales, I made my share of mistakes while learning the ropes. This book was born from a desire to share the insights and experiences I've accumulated throughout my career, aiming to help others avoid the same pitfalls. I've had the privilege of working directly with amazing clients, leading high-performing teams, and mentoring eager newcomers to the field. These experiences have given me a comprehensive understanding of the challenges and opportunities in technical sales. Throughout my journey, I've identified seven Timeless Behaviors that form the foundation of effective and meaningful interactions in presales. These behaviors—**Be Authentic, Listen Actively, Show Empathy, Have a Conversation, Practice Humility, Tell a Story,** and **Leave an Impression**—are not just theoretical concepts but practical strategies that I have personally relied on to achieve success. They have been instrumental in building trust, fostering relationships, and delivering value to clients.

Whether you're just starting your journey in presales or are a seasoned professional, this book offers valuable insights and actionable advice to enhance your skills and build stronger relationships with your clients and colleagues. The goal is to provide you with a roadmap to navigate the human side of technical sales with confidence and authenticity.

As you read through the chapters, I encourage you to evaluate your current approaches and consider how to incorporate these behaviors into your daily interactions. Authenticity, empathy, and effective communication are not just strategies—they are ways of being that can transform your professional and personal life.

Thank you for investing your time in this book. I hope it inspires, challenges, and equips you with the tools you need to achieve lasting success in our incredible profession.

– Ron Whitson

Acknowledgments

- ❖ First and foremost, I want to thank my brilliant and beautiful wife, Jana, who has encouraged me for many years to write this book. Your love and support continually motivate me. I love you!

- ❖ To Chris White, who has been an inspiration, friend, coach, and constant cheerleader throughout the process of bringing this book to life. Thank you, brother!

- ❖ To Shane Philips, who gave me my first opportunity to be a technical seller. Your trust and belief in my abilities set the foundation for my career in presales. Thank you!

- ❖ To my incredible kids and their significant others, affectionately known as "The Crew": Lacy & Alex, Cameron, Josh & Amy, Jarod & Chelsie, Jeremy & Jamie. Your love, encouragement, and laughter always lift me up. I am grateful to have each of you in my life. Keep pursuing big goals and ambitions—I'm proud of all that you achieve.

❖ To my dear grandchildren, Lucy, Harper, and Reid. You light up my life with your curiosity and joy. May you always chase your dreams and know that Pops believes in you.

❖ To all the amazing colleagues I have had the privilege of working with over the years. I express my deepest gratitude to each of you for contributing to my growth and learning in countless ways. Your insights, support, and collaboration have been invaluable, and I am honored to have learned from such a talented group of professionals.

❖ Thank you to all the friendly humans who have been part of my journey. Your influence and guidance have shaped my career and this book, and I am forever grateful.

Table of Contents

Dedication 5
What Readers Are Saying 7
Foreword by Shane Philips 11
Foreword by Brian Ivanovick 13
Preface 17
Acknowledgments 19
Table of Contents 21
About the Author 25
Chapter 1 – Introduction 27
    Understanding the Purpose of this Book 27
    How I Learned Presales 35
    Why do Technical People Struggle at Sales? 43
    Technical Ability, Business Acumen, and Soft Skills 46
    Introducing the Seven Timeless Behaviors 49
Chapter 2 – Be Authentic 53
    What does it mean to be Authentic? 53
    The Benefits of Being Perceived as Authentic 59
    Examples of Inauthenticity in Presales 62
    Story Time:
    Being a Friendly Human 68
    Suggestions to Develop Your Authenticity 71
Chapter 3 – Listen Actively 75
    What Does it Mean to Listen Actively? 75
    The Benefits of Listening Actively 78
    Techniques for Active Listening 79
    Story Time:
    An Overenthusiastic

    New Sales Engineer..84

    Suggestions to Develop Your Ability to
    Listen Actively... 89

Chapter 4 – Show Empathy..93

    What Does Being Empathetic Mean?...94

    The Benefits of Showing Empathy... 99

    Empathy and Diversity..101

    Story Time:
    Calling His Baby Ugly... 104

    Suggestions to Develop Your Empathy.. 111

Chapter 5 – Have a Conversation.. 115

    The Art of Conversing... 116

    Barriers to Conversing...123

    Story Time:
    Presenting With a Translator... 129

    Conversational Language Techniques...132

    Suggestions to Develop Your Conversational Style.................... 139

Chapter 6 – Practice Humility.. 143

    What Does it Mean to Be Humble?...144

    The Benefits of Being Humble... 148

    The Opposite of Humility... 149

    Story Time:
    A Humble Presales Professional.. 153

    Suggestions to Develop Your Humility.. 157

Chapter 7 – Tell a Story... 161

    What is Storytelling?... 161

    Storytelling Techniques...169

    The Benefits of Storytelling.. 177

    Story Time:
    A Few Stories from Down Under.. 178

Suggestions to Develop Your Storytelling Skill.................................185
Chapter 8 – Leave an Impression..187
    What Does it Mean to be Memorable?.....................................188
    The Benefits of Being Memorable...192
    Four Techniques for Delivering a
    Memorable Presentation..194
    Story Time:
    Krispy Kreme Donuts..203
    Suggestions to Develop Being Memorable.............................207
References...213

About the Author

Ron Whitson has dedicated nearly three decades to the dynamic world of presales, building a distinguished career as a sales engineer, solution consultant, direct seller, and leader. With extensive experience in leadership roles, Ron has not only excelled in his professional endeavors but has also made it his mission to mentor and guide the next generation of presales professionals.

Throughout his career, Ron has worked with a diverse range of clients, helping them navigate the complexities of technical sales. His deep understanding of the technical sales landscape, combined with his passion for fostering authentic client relationships, has made him a trusted advisor and respected leader in the field.

Ron holds a deep belief in the power of authenticity, empathy, and effective communication. His work aims to equip presales professionals with the tools they need to build meaningful connections, foster trust, and achieve lasting success in their careers.

When he's not working or writing, Ron enjoys working on his garden and playing tennis, which further enrich his well-rounded perspective on life and work. Ron currently resides in Roanoke, Texas, with his wife, Jana, and their pets, where he continues to inspire and lead by example in the ever-evolving field of technical sales.

> "The only way to do great work is to love what you do."
> – Steve Jobs

Chapter 1 – Introduction

Understanding the Purpose of this Book

Defining Presales

If you picked up this book, you likely already understand what people mean when they use the term presales. If you are unfamiliar with the term, allow me to provide some context, as it's important for the concepts and stories throughout the book. Even though presales has been around for a while, it remains an exciting profession that continues to evolve. I've been involved in presales for almost thirty years, and I delight that I can still learn and grow professionally. I genuinely love what I do!

For most of my career, I have been called a Sales Engineer. I've also had stints as a Solution Consultant and an Application Engineer, and there are countless other variations on the titles. The idea of having Solutions in our titles is something that is very much in focus currently and could represent a potential growth area for presales in the future.

Presales is a term used for the technical counterparts to the sales team. The salesperson is typically known as the Account Executive (AE) and has the overall responsibility for managing the opportunity and moving it toward winning the business—closing the deal. The job of presales is to convince buyers that our solution will solve the business challenges they are looking to address and drive the desired outcomes. This is often referred to as getting the technical win.

Presales professionals use several methods to achieve this. First, they ask buyers questions to understand the business challenge they want to solve, a process known as discovery. After completing discovery, the next step typically involves technically validating the solution, often through a product demonstration or "demo."

I dislike the word demo as I feel it demeans our profession in that it highlights a single component of our work. The demo is just the tip of the iceberg that most people see, while most of our work remains out of sight below the surface.

The format for presenting a product demonstration has changed significantly over the last few years. They once were just slightly removed from being a training session where the presales professional walked someone through a tutorial of the solution. Today's product presentations must be based on value and focused on the outcomes of successfully addressing the business challenges the buyer wants to solve.

Product demonstrations are a crucial component of presales activities. Several books delve into this subject, such as "Just F*ing Demo" by Rob Falcone and "Great Demo!" by Peter Cohan. Also, John Care's "Mastering Technical Sales" is a core textbook for our profession, offering valuable insights into improving presales skills.

For a broader framework beyond just product demonstrations, consider Chris White's "The Six Habits of Highly Effective Sales Engineers." This resource covers various aspects of the presales profession, providing practical tips for success. Whether your goal is refining your product demonstration skills or increasing overall presales expertise, these resources offer valuable knowledge to help you advance your career. While this book highlights techniques to make you a better presenter, it is not a how-to guide for demonstrating your product.

Since the beginning of presales, technical people have typically filled this role. One of the role's primary functions is explaining technical solutions to audiences who may be less technical in their understanding. The early presales professionals were technical resources who could crawl out of their basements and talk to other humans, or as I've heard it phrased, "they were the geeks who could speak."

I was definitely that geek early on, as I'll share later in this chapter. This book is a compilation of the lessons I've learned during my career in presales. While my technical abilities provided the entry point, true success and enjoyment in the role came from other skills that I had to develop. I hope this book helps you develop those skills and achieve lasting success in your presales role.

Achieving Success in Presales

Once you have a role in presales, how do you know if you are successful? There are really only two meaningful measures of achievement for our profession, and both of them can be tricky to properly measure.

1. Earning Trust of Sales Colleagues

If you'll excuse a sports reference, I've heard this referred to as "having the locker room." As in you either have it or you don't. When you have it, the salespeople you are collaborating with are comfortable working with you and will share that feeling with the other sellers. If you "lose the locker room," the opposite is true. Your sales counterparts won't have confidence in your ability to help them win the business, and you can count on the fact that they will share this opinion with the other sellers. If the sellers don't want to work with you, your time as a presales professional will be short.

It's critical to your long-term success to have the trust of your sellers. They need to believe that you are just as invested as they are in winning the business. They need to feel like they can trust you to say the right things around their prospects (and avoid saying the wrong things). I've found the best way to build and keep this trust and confidence is to have great relationships with the sellers I'm working with.

2. Establishing Trust with Buyers

Whether presenting your solution, responding to an RFP, or answering technical questions, you need your audience to trust you. As a presales professional, you need to earn the status of trusted advisor to your buyers. You know you've achieved this status when you can respond to a technical question with a simple yes or no, and that's all you need. Building this trust with your buyers is the second critical measure of success in presales.

You may notice that I didn't mention closing business or quota attainment. That's because those are well outside of presales' control. Of course, it's important to be able to win deals to be a successful presales professional, but the focus for presales should be on getting that technical win.

Whether it's gaining the trust of your buyers to secure the technical win or just being a great partner with your seller, both of these require the ability to build and manage relationships. There will be many different sellers and buyers with whom you will work throughout your career, and they will all have different temperaments and personalities. As I got into the role, I realized that the soft or people skills needed to develop those relationships would be essential for long-term success as a presales professional.

The Importance of Soft Skills

You can find many resources on the importance of soft skills, but I don't find that we call out the specific ones important to our presales role. As I worked through my career, I have identified seven **Timeless Behaviors** that have proven instrumental in my success. They are:

1. **Be Authentic**
2. **Listen Actively**
3. **Show Empathy**
4. **Have a Conversation**
5. **Practice Humility**
6. **Tell a Story**
7. **Leave an Impression**

In the subsequent chapters, we'll delve into these behaviors, exploring their significance and sharing anecdotes that illustrate their impact on presales success.

Who Should Read This Book?

I wrote this book for anyone in a technical sales role who wishes to improve and achieve success. It's written specifically for technical people working in a presales role who need to develop their ability to build and maintain relationships. I've put the book together to provide building blocks for developing these Seven Timeless Behaviors.

New Entrants to the Presales Role
People who are new to the presales role can benefit from my decades of experience and hopefully avoid some of the mistakes I made—you're welcome! Following the suggestions here can accelerate your career development and help you stand out from others in the role who may not be practicing the Seven Timelss Behaviors.

Mid-Career Presales Professionals
Those who have been in presales for a few years will benefit from reading the book. In my experience, the best presales professionals love to learn and grow, and let's face it, soft skills are an area often overlooked in professional training. Relationship-building is a critical component of our job. It should get some attention.

Presales Leaders and Managers
Finally, presales leaders are responsible for the growth and development of their teams. Presales professionals dedicate significant time to developing their product knowledge and honing their ability to deliver product demonstrations. It's about time we started focusing on developing the soft skills required in our jobs. I believe the Seven Timeless Behaviors can be an important program for improving the overall ability of their teams. And I know the team members will appreciate the investment in their professional growth.

In essence, this book serves as a comprehensive resource for individuals at various stages of their presales journey, offering practical guidance to elevate their skills and contribute to the success of their teams.

What Should You Expect to Gain from this Book?

You decided to invest in this book for some reason. It's only fair that I share some of the learnings you should expect to gain from your investment.

Understanding the Importance of Soft Skills

By the book's conclusion, you should have a deeper appreciation for the critical role that soft skills play in presales professionals' success. Recognizing their significance is the first step toward leveraging them effectively in your career.

Awareness of the Seven Timeless Behaviors

You'll learn how the Seven Timeless Behaviors can significantly enhance your effectiveness as a presales professional. These behaviors are fundamental tools for building rapport, fostering trust, and ultimately driving success in technical sales.

Recognition of Transferable Skills

Soft skills are transferable across any number of professional roles, and I would argue that they are more challenging to learn than some of the complex technical skills. Technology is constantly changing. During my time in presales, we've shifted from mainframes to the client-server architecture, and now we're all in the cloud— just a different application of client-server. Over the last few years, we've seen an explosion of artificial intelligence (AI) and large language model (LLM) applications. While the technology we work with is constantly changing, the Seven Timeless

Behaviors remain constant. Doesn't that sound like a worthwhile investment of your time?

Personal Growth Beyond Business
While this book focuses on professional development, mastering the Seven Timeless Behaviors can also enrich one's personal life. These skills can enhance communication, deepen relationships, and foster personal growth outside the workplace.

Entertaining and Insightful Stories
Throughout the book, you'll encounter anecdotes from my time as a presales professional. Some are shared to illustrate Timeless Behaviors, while others aim to entertain. These stories provide real-world context and practical examples to reinforce the concepts discussed.

Why Should You Listen to Me?

This book comes directly from my journey in presales. In the next section, I'll describe my early career, and you may find similar themes from your experience. It seems that most of us have had similar journeys in presales.

I leveraged my technical abilities as my entry into presales. I was doing a good job and getting praise from the sellers I worked with, but I realized something was missing. We had good meetings, and I delivered a solid product presentation, but we weren't consistently winning the business. I desired to be the presales person everyone wanted on their deals. To achieve this, I knew I needed to improve my soft skills.

As I started studying others who were successful in these areas, I began defining and documenting behaviors I wanted to develop in myself. These evolved into the Seven Timeless Behaviors, and as I started practicing and applying them, I immediately began achieving success. My overall win rate increased considerably, and I quickly became the "go-to" presales person for the sellers. I have stories where the company decided I needed to be on the other side of the planet to support an important deal.

Over time, my colleagues and peers have acknowledged that I embody these Timeless Behaviors. While this section may sound like boasting, it is intended to underscore why you should value my perspective on the subject.

Today, I spend a lot of time mentoring people new to presales. I believe it's vital for leaders to find ways to give back to our profession. I also have people on my team who are early in their careers. I've spent time with both groups, teaching them the Seven Timeless Behaviors and sharing why they are crucial to their success. Sharing lessons learned from your career with others is a wonderful feeling.

Practicing and championing the Seven Timeless Behaviors has anchored my journey from personal success to guiding others. I firmly believe that you will also gain valuable benefits from engaging with this book.

How I Learned Presales

My Name is Ron, and I'm a Geek

I do consider myself a standard-issue geek. I've always been interested in how things worked. As a child, this manifested with me taking many things apart. More often than not, I was able to put them back together. I don't think my parents were all that happy to come home one night and find I had decided to disassemble our landline telephone and connect it to my stereo system.

That innate curiosity continued into my teens. Personal computers were just beginning to be popular during my high school days. I remember taking a programming class on an Apple IIc. Our poor teacher was doing her best to read ahead of us and teach the class, but it was often a lost cause as my buddies and I were burning through the Turbo Pascal manual, learning how to program.

Writing code interested me as it was a way of creating something from scratch. You could code just about anything you could imagine. Curiosity, coupled with my early code-writing experiences, had a significant impact at one of my first jobs.

Story Time: How to Catch a Thief

One of my earliest jobs was managing a convenience store in Dallas for Stop-n-Go. They were a chain based out of Houston, Texas, with almost 1,000 stores in Texas, California, and Georgia. The stores had a computer in the back room that communicated Point of Sale (POS) information to the corporate office. The computer was a Tandy 2000 from Radio Shack. If you don't know, the Tandy 2000 had a superior processor to the other systems available then, but it just didn't catch on. It was the Betamax of computers. See also; Microsoft Zune, Laserdiscs, etc.

Chapter 1 – Introduction

Now, I wasn't supposed to be messing with this computer. Because of my curious nature, I started seeing what I could do with it and soon discovered it had Lotus 1-2-3, an early spreadsheet program. You need to realize this was the DOS-based version. People did everything with menu commands, and there was no mouse.

Staying a few hours after my shift was over here and there, I put together a simple spreadsheet that tracked sales and customer counts across the three shifts each day. It was a 24-hour operation, so there was the 7 am - 3 pm shift, the 3 pm - 11 pm shift, and the 11 pm - 7 am overnight shift. The spreadsheet calculated an average sale per customer and the percentage that each shift's sales contributed to the daily total. Over time, these average amounts and percentages per shift started showing patterns. People are creatures of habit, and the same people would typically stop by for their same snacks at the same time of day.

Part of our business process involved auditing the store. Simply put, a crew would come in, count every bag of snacks, every cup, and every lottery ticket, and compare that total to what the books showed. We expected some loss due to spoilage and other factors, but large variances usually led to serious consequences for the manager. One of my audits revealed a large variance. My district manager came by to discuss it with me, and that's when I brought up the spreadsheet.

After getting over his initial surprise and frustration that I was "tampering" with the corporate system, he started to see the benefit of what I had created. I showed him the shifts where the totals and averages were off the norms. They all happened during the shifts a particular employee worked. Some further investigation proved they were not ringing up some items and pocketing the cash.

The district manager was so impressed with this system I had created that he asked me to build a spreadsheet for every store in the Dallas—Fort Worth area and had the other managers call their numbers into me each day. My little spreadsheet ended up being a critical tool for monitoring fraud and theft across the stores.

Reflecting back, this was another formative experience for me. I was able to use technology to solve a business problem. I found this incredibly fulfilling, and it definitely left an impression on me and the district manager. It's fun to realize that this early illicit spreadsheet project on the computer in the back room set me on the course to where I am today.

The Road to Becoming a Sales Engineer

I ended up doing training for Stop-n-Go. New employees would come to the corporate office, where I would run classes to teach them what was taxable and what was not and how to operate the gas pumps. I enjoyed training people and sharing time with them.

I leveraged my training experience and spreadsheet skills to secure my next job as a software trainer. Being a trainer was a fantastic opportunity as I learned every software package they taught. I even wrote some software curriculum for them. After a year, they promoted me to Training Supervisor. Teaching new employees at Stop-n-Go was fun, but now I feel like a real professional. I'll never forget that one of our training facilities was at the intersection of Corporate (Drive) and Executive (Drive). Look, Mom—I made it!

My next career stop was a consulting firm. My first job there was providing spreadsheet support for several executives. I shared a cubicle with my buddy Ray Vera, who provided word processor support. We'd sit and wait for the phone to ring and then offer hands-on assistance.

Success led to more opportunities to learn and grow. I did some development in Visual Basic and then Visual InterDev, which became the .Net framework. I did everything hardware-related, from installing RAM (memory) chips on motherboards to running token-ring network cabling along the bottom of cubicle walls. I even did some account management, and that's how I got to know Shane Philips.

Shane worked with me on some accounts and got hired by a software company, MainControl. A year after he left, he called me up. It was October, 1998. I'll never forget what he said. "Hey Ron, there's this thing called a Sales Engineer. I think you'd like it, and I think you'd be good at it." It sounded almost too good to be true. I would get paid to work on a computer and talk to people, and if they bought our stuff, I'd make even more money. I took a leap and began my first job as a Sales Engineer.

SE See, SE Do

Yes. Presales existed in 1998, but it was still a young profession. There weren't professional organizations, training programs, or even that many books. John Care's "Mastering Technical Sales" was first published in 2002.

He told me one of the reasons for writing it was that he couldn't find any good resources for presales. His book was one of my earliest guides to the role.

Based on what I had seen people do at conferences, I had developed an idea of how I would present. As a developer, I regularly attended VBITS (Visual Basic Insider's Technical Summit). VBITS was a conference for developers where people showcased new controls they had developed and gave examples of how to code them. Almost every presenter followed the same format—they had some slides to set the context, then demonstrated the code or control. Some presenters were excellent and engaging, and some were not. This format became the model for how I would present as a Sales Engineer.

My training consisted of having that mental model in my brain while shadowing my colleagues and seeing how they delivered product demonstrations. My first goal was to replicate what they were doing and saying. This process was fine for learning the product and working out how to present it to others, but I quickly realized that I needed to find my own voice. Saying someone else's words did not sound like me. It was not authentic. I had to create my take on telling the stories, sharing the benefits of the solution, and communicating this technical information to my audience in a way that was authentic to me and believable for them.

This became easier as I developed confidence in the role, but I will not lie. My first product demonstrations were much more based on what I had learned as an instructor. I was going through and teaching the audience how to use the software. I wasn't trying to understand and solve their business challenges. I made plenty of mistakes early on.

Turning Mistakes into Learning

It's a good thing I was working for someone who understood that learning something new meant you would make mistakes. Like everyone else, I didn't enjoy the mistakes. I didn't enjoy feeling like I had failed at something. For those reasons, I made it a point to figure out what caused the mistake and then understand what I could learn from it. I wanted to implement a plan to mitigate the risk of that mistake happening again. This is how you gain wisdom, and going through the process can be difficult.

Selfishly, I started by focusing on aligning with my seller. I believed that if we agreed on the approach to the meeting and things didn't go well, they couldn't throw me under the bus. It was their plan, too! This meant working with them to establish a basic outline of what I would present and getting their sign-off on the plan.

We ended up having meetings that didn't go well even though we were aligned. That's when I learned it was important to have alignment with the audience. What are their expectations for the meeting? To address this, I put together a list of questions to ask before the meeting to discover those expectations. The questions helped me understand their goals for the meeting and what success looked like. These systems and processes helped to build confidence and drive consistency in my presentations.

What I have found over my time is that those who excel in the role and enjoy presales are typically people-pleasers. We want to make people happy, to make people like us, to please the sellers and our audience with the product demonstration we provide, to get a pat on the back afterward, and to hear people tell us they enjoyed the presentation and that we did a good job.

I was getting that in spades, but we weren't always winning the business. We weren't closing the deals it seemed we should be winning. It was about this time I realized I was a technical seller.

My Name is Ron, and I'm a Technical Seller

Wait! How did this happen? I don't want to be a salesperson!

Relax. You are a technical seller. There's a huge difference. You are not a used car seller. You are a highly trained technical individual tasked with conveying complex information to your audience in a way that will convince them to purchase your solution.

Chris White likes to say, "Selling is serving.", meaning that if you are doing the work of understanding the benefit to a company of solving a business problem and you help them to solve it, you are serving them much more than you are selling them on something. This concept can be a helpful model for technical people who bristle at the idea of being a seller.

I enjoyed the technical aspect of the job, and I was good at it. I wanted to be good at all aspects of the job, and as I started digging in on understanding sales processes better, one thing kept coming back to me. Sales is all about relationships, and if I wanted to get better at the job, I had to improve in building and maintaining relationships. All the technical ability in the world will not help you with relationships. For that, you need soft skills. I decided to identify those skills and work to improve them.

Chapter 1 – Introduction

Why do Technical People Struggle at Sales?

The Engineer Brain

Throughout my professional journey, I've witnessed many talented technical individuals struggle with the sales aspect of their roles. Much of this struggle stems from the wiring of our engineer brains. Engineers inherently gear towards problem-solving, preferring logical reasoning and efficiency over emotional considerations. They thrive in environments where they meet challenges head-on, relying on data and facts to navigate their decision-making processes precisely.

While engineers excel in their technical prowess, their comfort zone often revolves around technology and logic rather than the intricacies of interpersonal relationships and emotions. Ambiguity and uncertainty, always present in sales scenarios, can unsettle engineers accustomed to clear-cut solutions and tangible outcomes. Consequently, navigating the nuances of human interaction becomes a challenge, as engineers may need help to prioritize building rapport and understanding their clients' emotional needs.

Transitioning from a purely technical role to one that involves extensive client interaction can pose a significant challenge for many engineers. However, embracing this challenge and actively seeking growth opportunities can lead to remarkable development. By committing to continuous improvement and stepping beyond their comfort zones, engineers can adapt and develop the necessary skills for success. With time and dedication, the engineer brain can leverage its technical expertise to forge genuine connections with clients and achieve success.

Ultimately, the key lies in striking a delicate balance between technical ability and interpersonal skills, recognizing both as necessary components of a thriving presales career. To succeed in presales, engineers must actively develop their interpersonal skills to better understand and collaborate with their clients. They must learn to embrace the notion that they are a critical part of a sales team.

Selling as an Art

Every company I've worked for in a presales role has implemented a Sales Methodology. These methodologies constantly evolve, but the goal remains the same: creating a repeatable process for pursuing sales opportunities. The methodology creates consistency in the sales motion and helps the sales team avoid missing any important steps toward winning the business.

As much as companies try to operationalize sales, I believe it's more of an art than a science. Allow me to explain.

Imagine you have just created the perfect Sales Methodology. You have been able to document each step, from the first buyer engagement to contract signing. You've identified the needed resources to move to each sales stage appropriately. Do you believe you are going to close every opportunity using this methodology? No. Of course, you won't. But it's the perfect methodology. Why won't it always work? The answer is simple. It's because people are involved. Many times, buying decisions are based more on emotion than logic. Buyers come to trust and like one sales team over the others.

Now, consider plugging the engineer's brain into this scenario. We've got a technical person who is focused on answering technical questions and proving the solution while being less interested in building rapport with their audience. If this is the situation playing out in meetings, it's going to be a challenge to win the trust and favor of the audience.

Along with developing relationships with your buyers and building rapport, you must be familiar with their business. It's essential to speak their language and understand the types of problems they may face. For some solutions, having industry knowledge can be a requirement. Learn how to research a company to glean some of these details, and be sure to work with your sales counterpart. They probably already know some of this information.

I'm not suggesting that our technical presales engineers have to be the Picassos of Sales, but they must be able to recognize a paintbrush when they see one. For a presales professional to succeed, they must become familiar with sales processes, methodologies, and tools and recognize buying signals from their audience.

People Buy from People

The importance of building relationships is clear. As of the writing of this book, people are still buying from people. We haven't completely replaced everyone in the buying process with Artificial Intelligence (AI) yet.

Because people are involved in the sales process, it can get messy. You could be rolling along with a deal, expecting the close any day, and then out of the blue—BAM! Your buyer has had a change of heart and is now leaning towards another solution. This happens often and is just part of this crazy technical sales game.

You also cannot walk into a meeting and slap down your stack of technical certifications. That's just not the way it works. You have to earn the role of trusted advisor with your buyers. Regardless of the technology, ease of use, feature set, and many other factors, your buyers will decide who they trust and feel comfortable with. That's who they are going to buy from. It's your job to be that person.

To wrap up this section, engineer brains are wired not to want to invest time in building relationships with buyers. Buyers follow their hearts rather than their heads, ignoring the infallible logic presented by the presales professional. We cannot rely solely on our technical abilities to earn trusted advisor status. We have to actively work to build a relationship and prove our value to our buyers.

Technical Ability, Business Acumen, and Soft Skills

Technical Ability is Just One Area of Expertise

Successful presales professionals must possess three areas of expertise. It's also important to blend these areas properly, and we'll discuss that a little later in the chapter.

The first area of expertise is Technical Ability. Since people in presales typically have a technical background like I did, this area of expertise is likely an automatic checkmark.

Our technical abilities are where our confidence comes from when we present. We believe in ourselves as experts in our technical abilities and the solutions we represent. There are too many technical areas of expertise to list here, but consider things such as Structured Query Language (SQL), being able to code in Python or J-SON, or being able to set up and administer security applications.

Some of these programs may offer certifications that you can earn. Certifications are great, and I have earned more than a few, but they serve more to instill confidence in you than in your audience. The certifications you earn will build confidence in your ability to present from an informed position. This can help you establish yourself as an expert in the eyes of your audience and assist you in achieving that trusted advisor status.

But it's important to note that Technical Ability alone will not guarantee presales success, regardless of the number of certifications you earn. If we consider a presales professional with high technical ability but low soft skills, do you think they will be successful? My experience says they will have difficulty achieving success because their audience will perceive them as arrogant.

The Need for Business Acumen

Business Acumen is the second area of expertise essential for success in presales. I'm not saying you need an MBA, but basic knowledge of how businesses work. You must understand the differences between business-to-business (B2B) and business-to-consumer (B2C) transactions and speak the language of your buyer.

If you are meeting with a bank, don't talk about sellers. Banks call people in those roles bankers or advisors. If you show up talking about sellers, you will immediately lose credibility with the audience. Suppose you configure your demonstration environment for a meeting with a bank to reflect a medical insurance company. In that case, you tell your audience you understand nothing about their business.

The skills around researching your prospects and performing discovery are how you learn this critical information. You need to identify and understand the business challenges the company is facing. Once you know that, you need to work on tying that pain back to value. Be able to quantify the value they will realize by solving this problem.

Business acumen includes some basic business smarts. Let's assume you are selling a solution that will address their needs, and the price for your solution is half a million dollars. Let's further assume that the company could hire a new employee for about half of that amount and have that new person perform the task your solution provides. Your value proposition just got turned on itself and is no longer viable.

Business acumen alone will not guarantee success in presales. If we consider someone with high business acumen but poor or no soft skills, do we think they will be successful? Once again, they are likely to come across to their audience as arrogant.

The Need for Soft Skills

The final area is soft skills. We've seen repeatedly that people are at the heart of the sales process, so relationships are critical. Soft skills are how relationships are created and maintained, how you interact with others, and how people will remember you.

You may be familiar with this quote which has been attributed to Maya Angelou:

> "I've learned that people will forget what you said. People forget what you did. But people will never forget how you made them feel."

I've already shared quite a bit about soft skills in general, but I have found that people seldom write about the specific soft skills needed for presales success. I'm about to introduce you to the ones I think are critical for succeeding in presales, but let's cover one last example of blending these three areas.

Having great soft skills alone does not guarantee success in presales. Consider a presales person who has developed their soft skills well. They excel at building relationships and appear likable. Suppose they lack business acumen, perhaps because they are early in their career or they aren't very technical. How do you think their audience will perceive them? In this case, I worry more about the presales person because they might suffer from imposter syndrome. They might not feel confident addressing business or technical questions.

Having the proper blend of Technical Ability, Business Acumen, and Soft Skills is essential if you want long-lasting success in presales. The blend will vary from company to company and from job to job. Some highly technical solutions may require a presales professional with deeper technical expertise. Certain industries—pharma and financial—require a deeper understanding of the business regulations that those companies are subject to. A final variable to getting the perfect blend figured out is the audience. Presenting to an IT (Information Technology) crowd differs greatly from presenting to a Marketing team. The best presales professionals can adjust to meet their audience's needs.

Introducing the Seven Timeless Behaviors

Why I Believe They Are Essential

Throughout my career, I've seen way too many great technical people struggle to be successful presales professionals. Many times, they have the technical ability and the business acumen but lack the people skills. This was also the story of my early career. I knew there were skills I needed to develop. While I found a lot of great information on soft skills, I didn't see anything that called out the specific ones that would be most helpful in a presales role.

I started reading everything I could and studying others who were successful at these skills. I found sellers who were great at building relationships and asked them to share their secrets. When I noticed someone doing a great job practicing a soft skill, I would see what I could learn from them. Gradually, I developed my abilities in these areas, and my career started to skyrocket. I was the "go-to" person for the big deals, and sellers would ask to work with me on opportunities.

Over time, it has become clear to me that there are Seven Timeless Behaviors that presales professionals need to succeed. They are: **Be Authentic, Listen Actively, Show Empathy, Have a Conversation, Practice Humility, Tell a Story,** and **Leave an Impression.** I have worked to develop and strive to exhibit these behaviors daily. I am convinced that investing in learning and growing my skills in these specific areas has been the secret of my long-term success in presales. You will experience the same if you can learn and develop these.

1. **Be Authentic**
   When you are authentic, you are the most persuasive version of yourself. Allow your unique personality and charm to come through to your audience.

2. **Listen Actively**
   Active listening is how you make others feel heard. This is the first step in building any relationship, professional or personal.

3. **Show Empathy**
   Empathy is the ability to understand another person's perspective. This is the second step in building relationships.

4. **Have a Conversation**
   Conversing is two-way communication and involves actively listening. Passing information in one direction is called instructing.

5. **Practice Humility**
   Humility is the act of putting others before yourself. Approach others from a perspective of what you may learn from them, not what they can learn from you.

6. **Tell a Story**
   Storytelling is conveying information, ideas, or experiences in simple language using tools such as analogies, metaphors, and descriptive language. The best stories create emotional touch points for your audience.

7. **Leave an Impression**
   Being memorable to your audience means you made a lasting impression on them. This is due to the experience you delivered and how you made them feel.

The Behaviors Build on Each Other

An important concept to grasp as you read this book is that these behaviors build on each other and should be developed in a specific order. You might wonder why this sequence is crucial. Let me explain.

Start with the very first Timeless Behavior: **Be Authentic**. It's essential to find your own voice and point of view that resonates naturally with you and credibly with your audience.

Once you establish authenticity, the next step is to **Listen Actively**. If you listen attentively but your audience doubts your authenticity, your message will likely fall flat. See the connection?

Imagine you're being authentic and listening actively, but you're not showing empathy. This lack will hinder your ability to truly connect with the person you're speaking to. While I could elaborate on the remaining behaviors, the pattern should now be clear. Tackle them in the order presented to understand how each one influences and activates the others.

The subsequent chapters will explore each Timeless Behavior in detail. I will discuss why I consider each behavior crucial, and I'll provide examples of how failing to practice these behaviors can manifest in a presales context. Additionally, I'll share numerous stories from my experiences to underscore their importance. Each chapter concludes with specific suggestions for developing these behaviors further. Some recommendations include books to enhance your understanding, while others suggest activities to help you practice and strengthen these behaviors.

> "Be yourself;
> everyone else is already taken."
> – Oscar Wilde

Chapter 2 – Be Authentic

Welcome to the first Timeless Behavior. This is the proper starting point for this journey. You cannot develop the rest of the behaviors successfully without being authentic. Let's dive in and learn what it means to be authentic.

What does it mean to be Authentic?

Definition of Authentic

Let's start with defining what it means to be authentic. Here's what Mirriam-Webster has:

1. not false or imitation: REAL, ACTUAL
   an authentic cockney accent

2. true to one's own personality, spirit, or character
   is sincere and authentic with no pretensions
3. worthy of acceptance or belief as conforming to or based on fact
   paints an authentic picture of our society

I love the examples here, and I think they are in the correct order. Have you ever experienced someone who you believed was acting falsely? Do you know anyone who may, at times, seem untrue to their character or personality? Did you find those people worthy of acceptance? As a presales professional, it's your job to be believable. Being your true, authentic self is how you gain that belief from others.

Another measure of authenticity is the consistency you demonstrate between your inner values and outward actions. We all see people who are quick to give advice on how others should act and behave and then show the exact opposite behavior. There is a word for those people—hypocrites.

It may sound overly simplistic, but we should all strive for sincerity in our thoughts, words, and actions. Put another way, do what you say and say what you do. Set your compass to the values you hold for yourself, and then be intentional and consistent in how you demonstrate those values as you go about your life.

For example, if you value kindness, be kind to people. Make that your default setting when approaching others. Be the person who takes the shopping cart back to the store. Be the person who picks up the piece of trash that just missed the garbage can. Find opportunities to show the world what you value—even if the world isn't watching. This is how you align your actions to your values and demonstrate consistency.

I've noticed an interesting thing: my self-awareness has increased as I strive for consistency as an authentic person. I'm more aware of how I present myself and how I treat others. I enjoy being seen as authentic, and I don't want to do anything that would jeopardize that perception. I think of this as an extra filter through which I run things to ensure they align with my brand.

With introspection comes the need to embrace vulnerability. An authentic person tells the truth and puts themselves out there, even when it's uncomfortable. This honesty can sometimes create difficult situations. When this happens, it's crucial to understand how the issue arose, which may involve recognizing that you've done something inconsistent with your values. Vulnerability means accepting your mistakes or errors and learning from them.

Focusing on authenticity and aligning our actions with our values leads to more open and transparent relationships with others. There is no longer a need to "put on airs" when we're meeting people for the first time or worrying about impressing our friends when they come to visit. We are comfortable being our true, authentic selves, and we are ready for others to accept us as we are.

A Couple of Authentic People

I thought it would be helpful to provide a couple of examples of individuals who demonstrate the Timeless Behavior of authenticity. Sometimes, an example can be more powerful than a definition.

Brené Brown

Brené Brown is an American professor and writer who has spent over two decades researching and writing about courage, vulnerability, shame, and empathy. She has several books available, as well as videos and TED Talks. I enjoyed her books "Daring Greatly" and "I Thought It Was Just Me." Her TED Talk, "The Power of Vulnerability," remains among the most-watched.

As you read her books or watch her TED Talks, you experience the same person. She doesn't sugarcoat her life experiences. She puts it all out there and shares her feelings and frustrations with you as she deals with the same stuff we all go through. It would be pretty easy for an accomplished author and speaker to create that perfect persona for her audience, but thankfully, she does not. I believe Brené Brown embodies the Timeless Behavior of Be Authentic.

Tom Hanks

While everyone may not be familiar (yet) with Brené Brown, I'm pretty sure that's not the case with Tom Hanks. As one of the planet's most popular and recognizable actors, he's spent the last four decades entertaining us with both comedic and dramatic roles. With an estimated net worth of around $400 million US, it would be easy for him to fall into that trap of believing he's better than everyone else, but that just doesn't seem to be the case.

There are countless stories of Tom Hanks acting like a normal human being and showing incredible kindness to strangers. One of the most well-known stories happened in Rome when Hanks was filming "Angels and Demons." The movie production prevented a bride and her father from getting to the church for her wedding. When Tom heard what was happening, he immediately called cut and then went over and nervously tapped on the window of their limousine. He explained about the filming and then offered to escort the bride and her father to the altar. To this day, whenever he's around a wedding, he'll crash the party and offer to take a picture with the bride and groom. Tom just figures it's something they'd like and a great memory for their wedding day.

There are stories of him using his X, formerly Twitter, account to post items he's found to help return them to their owners.
Whether the stories come from everyday people or his celebrity friends, it just seems that everyone likes Tom, and he seems to like everyone. His consistent reputation for being a nice guy and his actions that bear this out make Tom Hanks an authentic person in my book.

The Value of Consistency

I think both Brené Brown and Tom Hanks enjoy getting to be themselves. That's what being authentic allows you to do. If you can maintain consistency in having your actions reflect your values, you just get to be you all day, every day. You don't have to worry about acting out a part—well, when Tom is working, he does, but that's a different story. Authentic people can express their true thoughts and feelings without worrying about inconsistency.

Your moral compass should drive your thoughts and feelings. It's essential to have that compass set to guide your day-to-day interactions. Establish the values you hold most dear and let them drive your decisions and behaviors. This consistency will help build trust in your exchanges with others and enhance your reputation as an authentic individual.

When you have the trust of the people you are working or interacting with, you no longer have to remember any stories you made up for them. Remember Jon Lovitz's pathological liar character from Saturday Night Live? If not, do a little online searching. You'll get a good laugh out of it. The character, Tommy Flanagan, just couldn't help himself. He'd build one outrageous lie on top of the next without worry. His catchphrase after making one of these outrageous claims was, "Yeah. That's the ticket!"

I'm sure you've encountered people like this personally and professionally. They don't seem happy with their reality and feel the need to add a little, so it's a better story than real life. I imagine those people struggle sometimes, as Tommy Flanagan would, with having to remember those extra details that were made up. When you consistently are your authentic self, you never have to worry about this.

While some people feel the need to fabricate a better story, others go to the next extreme and put on an entire show. They adopt the persona they think will impress someone over their true self. They become flexible in their beliefs to blend in with the current crowd. They let their internal compass spin wildly in an attempt to appear as something other than themselves. Being authentic frees you from having to play out a part. You get to be you.

No Hidden Agendas

When we are authentic in our interactions, we remove hidden agendas or ulterior motives. Our engagements become genuine and transparent without any concealed intentions or secondary purposes. Each interaction is approached with sincerity and honesty, grounded in a genuine desire to connect with others meaningfully.

Authenticity means engaging people without the sole purpose of personal gain or self-interest. Instead of looking only to extract value or benefits from interactions, authentic individuals approach each encounter with curiosity and openness, focusing on how they can contribute positively to the relationship. They prioritize mutual benefit and genuine connection over individual gain.

Embracing authenticity leads to more honest and genuine communication with others. When we align our actions and words with our true beliefs and values, we communicate authentically, without pretense or deception. This honesty cultivates deeper connections and fosters mutual respect and understanding in our interactions, creating an environment where meaningful conversations and relationships occur.

The Benefits of Being Perceived as Authentic

Being perceived as authentic offers numerous benefits that significantly enhance personal and professional relationships. When we present our true, authentic selves, we create a positive environment where honesty and sincerity are valued, reducing misunderstandings and conflicts. Moreover, being authentic boosts self-esteem, reduces stress, and promotes greater fulfillment and satisfaction. Here are a few of the benefits I've noticed from practicing the behavior of being authentic:

People Relate to You Easily

Authenticity has a remarkable ripple effect—it invites authenticity from others. Presenting ourselves authentically creates a safe and welcoming space for others to do the same. People feel more comfortable being themselves when they sense genuine sincerity in our interactions. This encourages them to open up and share their experiences more freely, leading to richer conversations and exchanges of genuine experiences.

Barriers to Communication are Reduced

When we embrace authenticity, we lower communication barriers by creating an environment of openness and honesty. This encourages others to reciprocate, leading to better understanding. Authentic communication builds trust, which serves as a catalyst for breaking down barriers, allowing dialogue and collaboration to flow freely.

Relationships Flourish More Quickly

Communicating authentically fosters quick rapport and strong relationships by encouraging attentive listening, clear expression, and meaningful conversations—this deeper understanding and connection leads to shared openness and honesty, building trust and mutual respect.

Increased Resilience

Embracing authenticity increases resilience by promoting self-acceptance and a realistic approach to life's challenges. Acknowledging and expressing emotions authentically cultivates emotional intelligence and self-awareness, essential for resilience. Authenticity encourages honest self-reflection, allowing us to confront difficulties directly and adapt effectively.

Enhanced Well-being

Being perceived as authentic enhances overall well-being by boosting self-esteem and self-acceptance. Aligning actions with true values builds self-confidence and strength, promoting integrity and reducing inner conflict. Ultimately, living authentically brings greater satisfaction and contentment, allowing us to pursue meaningful goals and relationships, resulting in a more fulfilling and satisfying life.

Is This Some Hippy-Dippy New-Age Guru Nonsense?

I'm not a guru, and in short, no. These are the true benefits I've experienced myself as a result of just being me—the true, authentic version of me. It was always there; I just needed to get much better about putting it (me) out there. Before I learned how to be comfortable being my true, authentic self, I tried being what I imagined others wanted me to be. Let me tell you, that didn't work.

I have noted these benefits as a carrot for you to lean in on developing this Timeless Behavior. I ask that you take on the challenge of defining your authentic self and then putting yourself out there, warts and all, for others to see and interact with. As you become comfortable doing this, I fully believe you will experience the benefits I've described. If you want assistance developing the behavior of authenticity, you can find some suggested resources at the end of this chapter.

Examples of Inauthenticity in Presales

Let's flip the script and discuss what happens when a presales professional is not authentic. These are not just examples from some book—oh, wait, they actually are. They were written by someone who has seen every one of the following examples played out in real life.

What I Want to Show You Versus What You Need to See

This first one unfolds daily in conference rooms and virtual meetings across the globe. In a way, it's hard to blame the presales professional for this one. We are well-intentioned people-pleasers who strive to deliver on the promise of a thorough and technically flawless product presentation. The biggest miss here is focusing the lens in the wrong direction.

Every meeting you deliver should focus on the prospect or customer you are speaking with. We'll delve deeper into this concept in **Chapter 6 – Practice Humility.** The critical thing to remember for now is that the focus of the meeting is not you. We love performing and having the spotlight, but everything you do should be in service to your audience.

You are in the meeting and presenting because the people in front of you have a need. They want some process in their business to be easier, cheaper, or more efficient. Your job is to fully understand what they are trying to achieve and then convince them your solution is the best way to address that need.

Oh. Did you think you were there just to deliver the demo?

That product demonstration is just one of several tools you have at your disposal to convince someone. I dislike using that short, four-letter d-word because it has become overused and receives too much attention. I like to think of the solution demonstration as an important prop I'll use at the right time along the buyer's journey. Done well, it can quickly advance a deal and earn champions who will fight with you to close the deal. But when a demonstration goes poorly, you create more work for yourself and delay the opportunity.

You aren't there to deliver a demonstration. You are there to help that prospective buyer solve their problem. If you were helping a friend or neighbor, would you show up with a bunch of slides and a slick demonstration? No. You'd learn what they are trying to fix, and then you'd talk with them to see if you can help them. If they need help picking up a ping pong table they just bought and you have a truck, you can provide value. If your mode of transportation is a motorcycle, you need to let them know you are not a good fit. We should have this same mindset when helping our prospective buyers.

No Small Talk

If you don't enjoy small talk, please raise your hand. If you are driving or if this would cause you to drop the book, you are excused from raising your hand and can just blink instead. You don't know this, but I just raised my hand as well. Small talk can be difficult, and I think our engineer brains are wired in a way that makes it not always easy for us to engage in it. The good news is that, like most skills, we can work on and improve it.

Start at the beginning with small talk and take the time to script out your introduction. There is never a time when it's not important to share brief introductions. If there are a large number of people and it would take too long for each person to give an introduction, consider just having the main speakers introduce themselves, and then others could do so if they have something to say or a question to ask.

Your intro doesn't have to be elaborate, but it should include your name and why you are in the meeting. My shortest introduction for the longest time was something like, "Hi, everyone. I'm Ron Whitson, and my job today is to show you how our solution can help you _____."
There have been a lot of different things filled in that blank over the years, but you get the idea—a quick, simple statement of your name and purpose. If you have a little more time, insert things like where you live or where you are joining from. People enjoy making connections based on shared experiences of where they have lived or visited. The introduction is your first step in building the relationship.

Can we talk about dating in a business book? Don't worry. I'll be careful. Do you know how, when you first start dating someone, you are completely dialed in on them? You want to know everything about them and find everything they say incredibly interesting. Yeah—try to do some of that when you make small talk at the beginning of those first calls with a new audience. Don't be inauthentic, but do show interest and curiosity.

Look for clues around the room or in a virtual meeting behind them on the wall. Can you connect (authentically) with anything? Is there something interesting that you could ask about? Do you see a book on their shelf that you enjoyed? I have a few old wooden tennis rackets on the wall behind my desk, which has prompted many conversations with people. Like my rackets, consider ways that you could provide hints to people about your interests. Make it easy for them to find a way to engage with you.

It's important to understand that there are safe subjects and some that are off-limits for a business call. If you are having a hard time finding topics for small talk, whip out the tried and true one-size-fits-all weather discussion.

It will always be hot, cold, rainy, snowy, or just weather-y somewhere, and we are all happy to talk about it.

I try not to have important meetings on Mondays, but that's always a great time to ask what everyone did over the weekend. And guess what? On Fridays, you can ask about upcoming weekend plans. The point is that the topics are not all that important. It's the ritual of small talk we need to understand and be able to perform.

I shouldn't have to mention that you should avoid political and religious subjects, but it's an important point, so I will. The risk of introducing politics or religion far outweighs any possible benefit you think it may derive. I was in a meeting once where a senior sales engineer tried to make a clever joke about a current political figure. It fell completely flat on the audience, and the feeling in the room changed immediately. This reaction took him out of his groove, and he never recovered.

Another potential whammy area is sports. Wait? What? Avoid sports? Yes. And for a straightforward reason. Only some people in your audience will be into the current sporting situation, and you run a bit of risk assuming that they are. I was on a panel recently with some incredible women presales leaders, and hearing their perspectives on the bro-sports culture was eye-opening. Now, that doesn't mean no women enjoy sports, but I think it's important to consider your audience and not just automatically assume they enjoy all the same interests as you do.

Remember to keep the small talk in moderation. After all, everyone in the meeting is investing precious time, and you don't want fifteen minutes of inane banter. Small talk has some value in planting the seeds for the relationships to bloom, but spending too much time on it can alienate your audience and make them feel like you are wasting their time. You can accomplish a lot of good by using the first five to seven minutes of the meeting for introductions and getting to know each other.

Faking Expertise

This message can be difficult for some technical sellers to receive, but you are not always the smartest person in the room. It's essential to recognize that everyone has expertise in different areas, and it's unrealistic to expect yourself to always have all the answers. Pretending to have knowledge you don't have is a sure way of losing credibility and trustworthiness with your audience. You should never feel the need to act like the smartest person in the room.

This is one of the quickest ways to lose the trusted advisor status. And believe me when I say that once you've lost it, regaining that status is incredibly difficult. There's an old saying that trust arrives on foot and leaves on horseback. What this means is that it normally takes some work to build up trust with another individual, but that trust can be lost in a single moment.

If you are asked a question and don't know the answer, just say so. Your audience will appreciate your honesty and authenticity. If the question concerns a subject you should know well, you risk damaging your credibility. If you attempt to fabricate an answer, that risk increases exponentially and forces you to remember the (made-up) answer you gave instead of just being honest and open. When faced with uncertainty, adopting curiosity can turn a potential setback into an opportunity for deeper exploration.

Be curious about the reason for the question and go into discovery mode. See what you can learn and what other insights you can uncover. Rushing to provide an answer without proper investigation can lead to misinformation and erode trust. In practical terms, employing techniques like the parking lot method can effectively manage unanswered questions, ensuring thorough follow-up and maintaining trust.

The "parking lot" method involves acknowledging unanswered questions or topics and deferring them for follow-up. The questions are "parked" somewhere—usually on a notepad or whiteboard. This approach demonstrates your commitment to providing thorough and accurate information while ensuring that no inquiries are left unanswered. Be sure to actually do the follow-up after the meeting. Share your findings with the audience to demonstrate your diligence and show that you care about their concerns.

Following a Script

I've never been a fan of scripts for demonstrations. The biggest reason is that you can only write a script for yourself. If anyone else tries to use your script, they are not being their authentic selves. They are trying to be you. Trust me, that's not going to work. Your audience will pick up on your discomfort, and worse, you will be so focused on reading the script that you will miss out on the conversation.

When presales professionals work off a script, they tend to follow it too strictly. If a question takes us off the beaten path, there's a push to get back to the script. This can limit your ability to address questions from your audience and cause them to lose interest in your presentation. Pushing to get back to your script tells your audience that their concerns are less important than your script.

Now that I've bashed using scripts let me go back and state that demonstration scripts are not all bad. A simple outline can help provide consistency in how a presales team showcases the product. I prefer outlines over detailed scripts as they allow the presenter to put their own words and personality into the presentation.

Your product presentation should be a conversation between you and your audience. **Chapter 5 – Have a Conversation** covers this in more detail, but two-way communication should happen during your demonstration.

Consider how these examples might make others perceive you as inauthentic. Have you ever committed any of the above? I have. But now I understand the importance of the Timeless Behavior of Being Authentic, and I strive daily to align my actions with my values, especially when presenting.

Story Time: Being a Friendly Human

Early in my career, I was not the best networker. The idea of keeping up with people who weren't on my team, didn't report to me, or didn't impact my work felt exhausting.

While some presales professionals dislike tradeshows, I always volunteered to cover our booth. I enjoyed delivering demonstrations at the booth, but I was ready to escape when they started wheeling out the bars for happy hour. I thrived in the spotlight while the booth was open, but once it closed, I wanted nothing more than to retreat to my room and recharge. I had done my job and didn't want to engage with anyone further.

A few years ago, I decided to combat my introverted tendencies by becoming more active on LinkedIn. I began by sharing my observations on the presales profession, aiming to offer unique and interesting insights. Since I dedicated time to creating these posts each Monday, I started using the hashtag #MondayMusings.

I was amazed by the reactions to my content and how quickly my network grew. I enjoyed creating posts, and people appreciated them. Soon, I began receiving requests from individuals seeking their first job in presales, wanting to hear about my experiences and ask questions. Managing these requests became essential, so I created a Calendly link to allow people to book time on my calendar. Immediately, emails started coming in, and I began having online meetings with the requesters.

A question asked all the time was what I looked for when hiring for presales. Based on my experience, four attributes tell me whether someone has the potential to be good at presales. They are:

1. Be a friendly human who can have a conversation
2. Have the grit for the grind
3. Be technically curious
4. Understand that you are in a sales role

The "friendly human" part seemed to stick with people. I believe I'm a friendly human, and I try to make sure my actions align with that concept. It's become an important part of my personal brand, and now you know how the book got its title.

Not long after I started these enhanced networking efforts, Mattie Stremic invited me to be a guest on the PreSales Collective Podcast. She was doing a series on Becoming a World-Class SC (Solution Consultant), and I joined her to discuss building your external network. Recording the episode with her was a great honor and a lot of fun.

During the podcast, Mattie commented that whether reading my posts or interacting with me through Slack or email, she definitely felt like I was coming across as a friendly human. When I heard her say that, it meant the world to me.

It's been quite a journey from the sales engineer who didn't want to put the effort into networking to someone recognized for it. I have been surprised by how my networking efforts have yielded so many benefits that I had not imagined: being invited to podcasts, delivering webinars, serving as a mentor, speaking at conferences, and many other wonderful opportunities. Through it all, I've tried to maintain my authentic self while being a friendly human. It seems to be working.

Suggestions to Develop Your Authenticity

I dislike the business books I've read that tell you what you should do but leave out the "how," so I thought it important to include suggested resources and activities to use as you develop the Timeless Behaviors.

Define Your Personal Mission

If you want others to perceive you as authentic, you must understand your beliefs and values. I think it's essential to take the time to write about these things and tie them to your personal and professional goals. You cannot make progress toward a goal if you leave it undefined. Putting pen to paper or typing words on a screen can be a powerful and enlightening exercise.

Along those same lines, can you verbalize the "why" behind your actions? Do you understand what drives you? My "why" has changed throughout my career. Early on, a desire to excel in the role and be recognized as an expert drove me. I wanted to be the "go-to" Sales Engineer for the largest, most critical deals. My "why" has now shifted to giving back to this profession that has engaged me for almost three decades and provided for my family. I enjoy mentoring the next generation of presales professionals and watching their growth. Do you know what drives you?

Consider taking your values, beliefs, goals, and your "why" and putting it all together into a personal mission statement. Here's an example, *"To empower and inspire others to reach their fullest potential in presales through sharing experiences and meaningful connections. I strive to lead by example, fostering environments of inclusivity, growth, and positivity, where individuals can thrive and make a difference in their own lives and the lives of others."* Sound like anyone you know? Your personal mission statement can be powerful in helping to define what the authentic you is all about.

Once you have your personal mission statement, start looking for ways to implement it in your daily professional life. In other words, walk the walk. If you are driven by helping others, look for ways to be helpful at work. Find someone earlier in their career and reach out to learn about them and share your experiences. If your company has service organizations or volunteer opportunities, take advantage of them. Find ways to activate your personal mission.

Seek Feedback from Trusted Sources

Feedback is a gift, but let's be honest. Not all feedback carries the same worth. It's important to consider the source of the feedback and their potential motivations. I've been on interview panels where a prospective hire delivered a demonstration as part of the application process. In one example, it was clear that a panelist had never delivered a demonstration before, and the feedback they shared seemed inaccurate. It's important to consider who you trust to provide accurate, candid feedback.

While individuals in your management line may provide valuable feedback on job performance or specific tasks, seeking feedback on authenticity requires a different approach. Establishing a closer connection with someone who can provide candid insights into your behaviors and interactions is essential. Consider selecting a trusted peer or mentor who understands your professional journey and with whom you feel comfortable openly sharing your authenticity goals. This person should possess the experience and knowledge to offer meaningful feedback tailored to your development in this area.

Be transparent with your selected feedback source about your intentions and objectives for seeking feedback. Communicate what aspects of your authenticity you aim to develop and improve. Sharing any previous feedback you've received from others can provide context and help identify specific behaviors you may need to address. Establishing this open dialogue ensures that you and your feedback provider are aligned on the goals of the feedback process, fostering a constructive and supportive environment for growth.

Embrace the feedback you receive as a valuable gift intended to support your personal and professional development. Recognize that soliciting feedback demonstrates your commitment to growth and improvement. Approach the feedback with an open mind and a willingness to consider alternative perspectives. Remember that feedback is not a judgment but an opportunity for learning and growth. Emphasize your gratitude to your trusted feedback provider for their time and insights, reinforcing the collaborative nature of the feedback process.

Growth won't happen unless you take action based on what you learn from the feedback. This needs to be an iterative process. You will not learn everything and fix everything in one round of feedback. Work towards incremental improvement and progress. Consider setting a regular cadence with your trusted source.

As you meet and follow up, review the goals and the progress you've made. Share any concerns or struggles. Being uncomfortable can be a sign of growth. It can also be a sign of indigestion, but let's stick with growth for now. As you progress along your career path, it may be necessary to find new sources to provide trusted feedback, and there's no rule that says how many you need.

Journal to Uncover Your Motivations

Journaling can serve as an effective tool for understanding your motivations and reactions as you work to develop authenticity. You can journal during a reflective time and share your entries with a trusted source for feedback. Many people who journal let their stream of consciousness flow when writing, but if you need prompts to get started, here are some suggestions:

1. Describe a situation you faced and your response
    a. Did you rely on your moral compass?
    b. Did your reaction reflect your values?
    c. Was your focus on self or the other?
2. Thinking about this situation
    a. What was your motivation for your response?
    b. What would you have done differently?
    c. Did you live out your personal mission?

Use these prompts as they are or as jumping-off points. The magic in journaling is the writing itself and the personal reflection it can drive.

"We have two ears and one mouth, so we can listen twice as much as we speak."
— Epictetus, Greek Philosopher

"The art of conversation lies in listening."
— Malcolm Forbes

Chapter 3 – Listen Actively

Before we move on to the next behavior, I have to ask: Do you believe you are showing up every day as your true, authentic self? Remember that the Timeless Behaviors build on each other, and even if you are a world-class active listener, it's all for naught if you are not being perceived as authentic.

What Does it Mean to Listen Actively?

There are plenty of articles and some great books on the art of listening actively. I've got one mentioned at the end of this chapter as a resource for developing this Timeless Behavior in yourself.

Reflect on the good listeners you know in your life. Have you ever considered what those individuals are doing that makes them effective listeners? I have, and even though these qualities often appear straightforward, they are crucial to mastering active listening.

Putting Effort and Focus on What Someone Says

We've all been in a situation where we're engaged (stuck) in a conversation with someone and are struggling to pay attention to what they are saying. They sound like the teacher from the Peanuts cartoons, "Wah wah wah-wah-wah wah." Or worse, have you ever been conversing with someone heads-down, preoccupied with something on their phone?

Effective active listeners can focus and direct attention on the speaker. They listen to what the speaker is saying and observe nonverbal cues.

Understanding the True Message

Admit it. There have been times when you engaged in a conversation with someone and immediately afterward didn't clearly recall what was discussed. Too often, we let our feelings or prejudices color our perception, causing us to miss hearing (and understanding) the true message the speaker intended to convey.

Effective active listeners set aside personal biases and listen without preconceived agendas, ensuring they grasp the speaker's intended message. They create an environment where others feel comfortable sharing openly.

Giving Verbal and Non-verbal Feedback

In that first situation where you found yourself trapped into listening to an unending story, you likely provided feedback to the person telling the story. It's also likely that this feedback was not thoughtful but something you did in an attempt to hurry the story and facilitate your escape.

Effective active listeners provide verbal feedback to indicate agreement and understanding. They also share nonverbal feedback with the speaker in a way that encourages them to continue sharing.

Most Respectful Interpretation

Human beings are pre-wired with many complex emotions, and it's normal for those emotions to bleed into our professional lives. Our emotions can create situations where we interpret the information we receive differently than intended—and, in some cases, more negatively.

Effective active listeners practice the most respectful interpretation, assuming the best intentions in communication. When clarity is needed, they ask direct questions to ensure understanding.

Story Time:
A Short Story on Distractions

A few years back, when regular in-person meetings were the norm, I had a manager who regularly showed me how important I was to him during our one-to-one meetings by putting his phone face-down on the table while we were meeting. During our time together, he occasionally checked his phone or looked at his watch. While I appreciated his time with me, I didn't always feel like I had his full attention.

During that same time, I had a recurring meeting with the lead of another department. We worked closely on a few projects, and staying in synch was important. During our meetings, she put her phone away. She never pulled it out to check it. It remained out of sight during our entire meeting. That person showed they were paying attention to me and that our time together was important. She actively worked to eliminate distractions.

The Benefits of Listening Actively

With an understanding of what it means to listen actively, let's move on to some benefits of demonstrating this behavior. As you read on, understand that these are benefits I experienced in my career through developing my active listening skills.

Makes the Other Person Feel Heard

Active listening fulfills a fundamental human need for acknowledgment and understanding, enhancing connections through attentive engagement and validating others' experiences. Individuals build trust and promote productive interactions by listening actively and making the other person feel heard. This approach supports innovation and practical problem-solving, which are crucial in presales and beyond.

Demonstrates Understanding

Effective communication relies on both transmitting and accurately receiving messages. Active listening ensures understanding not only the speaker's words but also their emotions and nuances, increasing clarity and reducing misunderstandings.

Removes Barriers to Communication

Active listening removes barriers to effective communication by addressing distractions, biases, and emotions that hinder understanding. Distractions or interruptions disrupt focus, while biases and strong emotions like anger or fear can distort interpretations. By practicing active listening techniques, individuals can identify and mitigate these barriers, ensuring better comprehension and creating an environment conducive to meaningful and respectful dialogue.

Creates a Collaborative Environment

Active listening supports open communication by encouraging individuals to express their thoughts and concerns freely, leading to more productive conversations. By creating a supportive environment where everyone's voice is respected, active listening lays the foundation for collaboration.

Techniques for Active Listening

Earlier in the chapter, we reflected on the good listeners in our lives and some of the things they did that made them effective active listeners. Let's go deeper into some of the techniques for listening actively.

Focus Completely on the Speaker

Focusing on the speaker is much easier when you can remove distractions. This means eliminating anything that may pull your attention away. Our phones and electronic devices are great for keeping us connected, but the constant notifications of emails, texts, and app alerts pull our focus away from the task at hand. Regaining that focus takes time.

It's also essential to eliminate any mental distractions. Be present in the moment, and don't let other issues or worries interfere with your ability to listen actively to the speaker. Be mindful of your emotional state so you can manage these influences.

As you listen, be sure to maintain eye contact. It's a powerful nonverbal cue that communicates attentiveness and interest in the speaker's message. By maintaining consistent eye contact, active listeners convey respect and engagement, building a sense of connection and understanding between both parties.

You can further demonstrate understanding by offering both verbal and nonverbal feedback. Verbal feedback can include phrases like "I see." or "Go on." to indicate understanding and encouragement. Nonverbal feedback, such as nodding, leaning in, or facial expressions, also plays a crucial role in conveying attentiveness and comprehension. Be careful not to overuse feedback, as it can be seen as inauthentic.

You should also pay attention to the speaker's nonverbal cues. Their body language, gestures, and tone of voice can provide valuable insight into their emotions and intentions. Active listeners carefully observe these cues to better understand the underlying message and respond appropriately.

Taking notes during a conversation can help active listeners retain key information and demonstrate their commitment to understanding the speaker's message. While it's important not to let note-taking distract from active listening, jotting down important points can help you process and recall information later. You can use those notes to recap the conversation and ensure you received the message correctly.

Don't Interrupt no Matter What

The absolute quickest way to convey to someone that you are not listening to them is to interrupt them. Always allow the speaker to finish a thought, and don't interrupt them no matter what. It doesn't matter how enlightening your contribution may be. The act of interrupting does so much damage that it's simply not worth committing.

When they pause, be ready to do one of a few things: give an affirmative response to indicate understanding, summarize what you heard and check for understanding, or ask a clarifying question. And then—you guessed it—allow the speaker time to thoroughly answer without interrupting them or trying to finish their sentence for them. As presales professionals, we are intelligent individuals, and you likely understand the question someone is getting ready to ask, and you likely know the answer. The difference between a good and great presales professional is avoiding interrupting the speaker before sharing the answer.

Sometimes, you are ready to ask a question or share information while someone is speaking. Having discussed the detrimental effects of interrupting someone, how do you indicate you would like to say something? Subtle cues such as raising a hand or gently nodding can signal readiness to contribute. Using one of these cues, the listener demonstrates their engagement in the conversation while respecting the speaker's turn to speak.

Developing the art of not interrupting others is fundamentally a lesson in patience. It demands the discipline to momentarily withhold your thoughts and responses, giving the speaker the uninterrupted space to convey their message.

Repeat a Summary and Ask If You Have it Right

Active listening aims to ensure an accurate understanding of the message. A helpful technique involves finding opportunities to paraphrase what you've heard to confirm comprehension. Your notes may be beneficial when summarizing key points back to the speaker.

When you can speak without interrupting the speaker, share the key points you've heard or written down and then ask if you have it right. That exchange may go something like this in a presales situation:

Presales Professional - *"Thank you for that, Don. What I just heard was that your team is responsible for getting marketing materials for new products to the sales team during that two-week window before the product launches. Did I get that right?"*

If you missed any details, the speaker should let you know. Apologize and inquire about what you missed or misunderstood. After receiving additional information, summarize again and confirm your understanding. Whether this information informs technical responses or sets the stage for a future product demonstration, it's crucial to capture it accurately while ensuring the speaker feels acknowledged.

Listening to Understand Versus Listening to Respond

One of the most valuable lessons I've learned is the distinction between listening to understand and listening to respond—a concept that's deceptively simple yet profoundly impactful.

Think about the last time you were in a disagreement, big or small. Were you actively listening to understand the other person's viewpoint and emotions, or were you focused on crafting your rebuttal? In my experience, disagreements often devolve into a quest to counter the other person's point rather than grasping their perspective.

In popular culture, characters often deliver witty comebacks or clever retorts during arguments, aiming to 'score points' rather than engage in genuine dialogue. This approach sharply contrasts with active listening, where the primary focus should be understanding the speaker's message.

When we fall into this situation, we miss the true message the speaker is trying to convey. Sadly, this dynamic plays out in interactions between business people all over the world every day. We've closed ourselves off to receiving and understanding the message.

A practical way to assess your active listening skills is to reflect on your intentions during conversations. Consider whether you are genuinely listening to understand the speaker's message or if your focus is primarily on preparing your response. This differentiation is critical because listening to understand entails fully engaging with the speaker's perspective, emotions, and intentions, whereas listening to respond may prioritize your own agenda or viewpoints.

Story Time: An Overenthusiastic New Sales Engineer

During my time in presales, I've had the privilege of hiring and coaching many newcomers to the role. Everyone came to the profession with their own gifts and abilities and areas needing further development. My job as a coach and leader was to foster an environment where their talent could flourish, and we could work on improving the areas where they needed to grow.

I remember one young sales engineer I brought onto the team. Let's call him Michael. Michael had a solid technical background and was incredibly eager to break into the world of presales. He was excited to join our team and determined to become a standout sales engineer.

Since his technical abilities were solid—he came to us from professional services and knew the product well—our coaching sessions were more about his demeanor and style when presenting to a prospect. Like most engineer brains, his was wired to move quickly and expect his audience to keep up with him. I knew his weakest area was active listening, which would be his Achilles' heel in a prospect meeting.

The day arrived for Michael to have his chance to present to a prospect. I identified a small opportunity that

Chapter 3 – Listen Actively

provided minimal risk if something didn't go as planned. I gave Michael a ton of credit for his preparation and practice. He created a great story that tied the prospect's business challenge to an outcome and had relevant case studies to reference. His click-path for the demonstration was solid, and our dry run went off without a hitch. He was as ready as he could be, but I had concerns about whether his active listening skills would manifest...or not.

This was an on-site meeting at the prospect's location—I know, real old school, right? We performed one more quick run-through at the hotel the evening before, and we all felt comfortable with our agenda and Michael's story.

We got set up the next day in the prospect's conference room. All the technology for connecting and presenting worked perfectly. The account executive started the meeting well, confirming the challenges we had previously uncovered and setting the stage for the solution demonstration.

It was time for Michael's big premiere! He started a bit too fast initially, likely due to nerves, but recovered and settled into a good groove a few minutes in. Things were going well and according to plan.

About fifteen minutes into the demonstration, a potential user of the system, Barb, had a question about some of the fields on the request form. This form was how end users submitted a request into the system. This question often came up during meetings and was easy to answer.

The exchange went something like this:

> **Barb** - *"The form we are currently using has fields for the user's department and other—"*
>
> **Michael** - *"Don't worry about the fields! Our form is configurable and can have whatever fields you need. These are just my demo fields."*

Yep. He interrupted her—just started talking before Barb even finished her sentence.

Michael was trying to be helpful, but his actions were different from what came across. Instead, he was perceived as arrogant and uncaring. Is this fair? It doesn't matter. That's how his actions made Barb feel.

I tried to intervene without throwing off the flow of the demonstration by asking Barb to share more about the fields on their current form. She opened up and shared a little about the form and their process. I wanted Michael to pick up on what I was doing and remember some of our work around active listening. Sadly, his eagerness to please caused him to continue interrupting and talking over his audience a few more times that day.

We finished the meeting and discussed the following steps to set up. They were still interested in our solution, but their experience of not feeling heard meant we had work to do to rehabilitate our position and our chance to win the business.

The following week, our champion provided negative feedback to the account executive. As expected, it focused on the demonstration and the perception that we didn't listen to them.

Michael was unaware of the challenges he created for himself and the company by not listening actively. He left the meeting believing he had done a good job on the demonstration. To be fair, he prepared and delivered well, but he failed to listen actively.

That afternoon, I found myself at the airport with Michael, and we had time to grab dinner before our flights. When I asked Michael how he thought he did, he expressed satisfaction with his preparation and delivery. I agreed, then inquired about how often he had interrupted his audience. After a brief pause, realization dawned on him, and his expression fell. The impact of his actions during the meeting hit him at that moment, and he was dismayed that he had let me down.

Learning and growth come from painful moments like these. It's how you gain experience and wisdom. I'm pleased to say that Michael used that moment as a catalyst for professional development. He sought out articles on the subject and read constantly on how to be a better listener. He asked other team members to share their tips and tricks and worked at incorporating those techniques. It didn't happen immediately, but Michael became an excellent active listener because he worked at it.

A Friendly Human in Presales

Notes

Suggestions to Develop Your Ability to Listen Actively

Like the previous chapter, I believe it's important to provide some resources for you should you decide to work on developing your ability to listen actively.

Be Mindful During Your Next Opportunity to Listen

Like almost every skill or ability, it will take effort and practice to develop. The next time you are in a situation where you need to listen to someone actively, try to do the following:

- **Remove distractions.** Silence your phone and put it away. Turn on Do Not Disturb on your computer to avoid notifications for email or Slack.
- **Be present.** Take the time to reset and focus on the task at hand mentally. If there is too much going on to be present, consider rescheduling the meeting.
- **Pay attention to non-verbal cues.** You may be surprised by the additional details you pick up when you are completely present and not distracted.
- **Practice non-judgemental awareness.** Work at listening to understand and remove the filters and prejudices that distort your perception of the message.

You likely won't see changes overnight, but implementing these techniques can enhance your listening skills and foster better understanding and communication in your interactions. Consider journaling about your progress along the journey.

Practice Delaying Your Response

For some people, silence is awkward. They need to fill the space with words. That is not active listening but more about wanting to hear your own voice versus understanding others. Consider working on being comfortable with the pause and having space in the conversation. If you need help with learning how not to respond immediately, try the following:

- **Pause and breathe.** Give it a beat, and just let the moment be still. Silence can be an effective tool for conveying thoughtfulness.
- **Repeat what was just said.** This is a way of buying some time for your brain to work on an appropriate response.
- **Count to ten.** Silently count from one to ten in your head. Many times, others will fill in the silence, which could provide another viewpoint to consider.

Book Recommendation:
I Hear You - by Michael S. Sorensen

I highly recommend this book for anyone looking to enhance their listening skills. Although it's often categorized as a relationship book rather than a business guide, its insights into effective communication are invaluable in any context. Sorensen delves into the art of active listening, offering practical strategies and real-life examples to help readers understand the profound impact of truly hearing others. I found numerous nuggets of wisdom in this book and have frequently suggested it to colleagues and friends alike as a powerful tool for gaining a deeper understanding of active listening and its transformative effects on interpersonal relationships and professional interaction.

Notes

> "If there is any one secret of success, it lies in the ability to get the other person's point of view and see things from his angle as well as your own."
>
> – Henry Ford

Chapter 4 – Show Empathy

At this point, we've covered the first two Timeless Behaviors: **Be Authentic** and **Listen Actively**. Let me stress once again that it's important to develop these behaviors in order. It's difficult to show empathy to someone if you are unable to listen actively. Once you have practiced these first two, we can layer in the third Timeless Behavior, "Show Empathy."

Empathy is a significant skill to develop. While some argue that empathy is an innate behavior that you are either born with or not, it can be learned and mastered. Each of us has the capacity to empathize with others; it's simply a matter of honing this skill like any other. With practice and conscious effort, anyone can become more empathetic in their interactions.

What Does Being Empathetic Mean?

Being in the Other Person's Shoes

One of the simplest explanations of empathy is to imagine what it would be like to experience someone else's perspective. It's a beautiful thought exercise but one that is difficult to do. When done correctly, we must set aside our biases, assumptions, and values to truly understand the other person's point of view. Empathy requires we consider their thoughts, emotions, and experiences without filtering them through our interpretations.

Cultural differences play a significant role in shaping how individuals perceive the world around them. What may seem logical or acceptable in one culture could be entirely different in another. Recognizing and respecting cultural nuances is crucial for developing empathy and bridging understanding between people from diverse backgrounds.

Educational backgrounds also influence how individuals perceive and interpret information. Someone with a background in psychology may approach a situation differently than someone with a background in engineering. Understanding these differences can help us appreciate varying perspectives and communicate more effectively.

Differences in background include various aspects such as upbringing, socio-economic status, and family dynamics. These factors shape our values, beliefs, and attitudes, influencing how we perceive the world.

A variety of experiences further contributes to empathy's complex nature. Each person has encountered different challenges, triumphs, and setbacks, shaping their emotional responses. Empathy requires us to consider these diverse experiences and empathize with the emotions they evoke.

Being in another person's shoes simply means acknowledging and accepting that others have a perspective different from yours, shaped by their culture, values, education, upbringing, and personal experiences. When we successfully show empathy, we demonstrate that we appreciate their perspective.

Poetry Time: Judge Softly

You have probably heard the phrase, "Walk a mile in another person's shoes." The full quote is, "Before you judge a man, walk a mile in his shoes." It's been credited to Native American culture but is most likely from a poem written in 1895 by Mary T. Lathrap titled "Judge Softly."

Pray, don't find fault with the man that limps,
Or stumbles along the road.
Unless you have worn the moccasins, he wears,
Or stumbled beneath the same load.

A Friendly Human in Presales

There may be tears in his soles that hurt
Though hidden away from view.
The burden he bears placed on your back
May cause you to stumble and fall, too.
Don't sneer at the man who is down today
Unless you have felt the same blow
That caused his fall or felt the shame
That only the fallen know.

You may be strong, but still the blows
That were his, unknown to you in the same way,
May cause you to stagger and fall, too.

Don't be too harsh with the man that sins.
Or pelt him with words, or stone, or disdain.
Unless you are sure you have no sins of your own,
And its only wisdom and love that your heart contains.

For you know if the tempter's voice
Should whisper as soft to you,
As it did to him when he went astray,
It might cause you to falter, too.
Just walk a mile in his moccasins
Before you abuse, criticize and accuse.
If just for one hour, you could find a way
To see through his eyes, instead of your own muse.

I believe you'd be surprised to see
That you've been blind and narrow minded, even unkind.
There are people on reservations and in the ghettos
Who have so little hope, and too much worry on their minds.

Chapter 4 – Show Empathy

*Brother, there but for the grace of God go you and me.
Just for a moment, slip into his mind and traditions
And see the world through his spirit and eyes
Before you cast a stone or falsely judge his conditions.*

*Remember to walk a mile in his moccasins
And remember the lessons of humanity taught to you by your elders.*

*We will be known forever by the tracks we leave
In other people's lives, our kindnesses and generosity.
Take the time to walk a mile in his moccasins.*

Avoiding Judgement

When showing empathy, we must avoid imposing our values onto others. Genuine understanding exists when we respect diverse perspectives and refrain from forcing our beliefs onto those we interact with.

Creating a safe space for sharing these viewpoints is fundamental to the practice of empathy. Within such an environment, individuals feel empowered to express themselves without fear of judgment. Cultivating trust and mutual respect establishes an environment where individuals can openly share their thoughts, emotions, and experiences, leading to deeper understanding.

Developing empathy requires us to embrace vulnerability. By modeling vulnerability ourselves, we create a culture that values honesty and transparency, inviting others to share their vulnerabilities without fear of judgment. This culture of openness strengthens bonds and cultivates empathy by allowing individuals to relate to one another on a deeper level.

Empathy also serves as a catalyst for personal growth and transformation. We facilitate self-awareness and understanding by encouraging individuals to reflect on their experiences, explore different perspectives, and learn from their interactions with others. Promoting personal growth fosters compassion, empathy, and resilience, empowering individuals to become more empathetic and compassionate.

Approaching Others From a Supportive Perspective

When interacting with others, it's beneficial to approach them with a mindset of what we can learn from them. Being open-minded allows us to recognize each person's unique insights and experiences. By seeking to understand their perspective, we not only demonstrate empathy but also enrich our own understanding.

Rather than making assumptions or judgments, cultivating a genuine interest in the thoughts, feelings, and experiences of others can lead to more meaningful interactions. Asking open-ended questions and actively listening to their responses can help uncover valuable insights and create space for empathy.

When others experience moments of need, we must consider what we can do to support or help that person. Whether offering a listening ear, providing practical assistance, or simply being present, demonstrating a willingness to help can make a significant difference in someone's life. Sometimes, a person needs a kind word, a reassuring gesture, or a compassionate presence to feel understood and supported. By offering comfort in times of distress or uncertainty, we demonstrate empathy and show that we are there for them.

The Benefits of Showing Empathy

Let's investigate some of the benefits empathetic individuals may recognize. As you read through these, imagine how these benefits will present themselves in your career as a presales professional.

Enhanced Communication

Empathy in communication drives true understanding by encouraging active listening and seeking to comprehend others' perspectives and emotions. This creates a basis for meaningful dialogue where individuals feel heard, valued, and respected. Additionally, empathetic communication involves interpreting non-verbal cues, often conveying emotions and intentions more accurately than words. By recognizing these cues, individuals can facilitate more authentic interactions. Empathy also cultivates compassion and respect, leading to a culture of mutual understanding and stronger interpersonal connections.

Increased Trust

Showing empathy in relationships creates emotional safety, encouraging individuals to trust and open up without fear of judgment. Trust builds a foundation for honest, authentic communication. Demonstrating sincerity through genuine concern for others' well-being builds trust and credibility as people recognize and appreciate our intentions. By being transparent and honest about our thoughts and feelings, we cultivate trust, making us reliable partners in communication.

Stronger Relationships

Empathy strengthens relationships by enhancing communication dynamics and increasing mutual understanding. By actively listening and empathizing with each other's perspectives and emotions, individuals build trust and respect. Empathy also creates a sense of connection and support, making individuals feel understood, valued, and supported, which enriches their bonds.

Reduced Conflict and Tension

Empathy is crucial in reducing conflict and tension by validating emotions, promoting perspective-taking, and empathy-driven solutions. When individuals feel heard and understood, they are less likely to escalate conflicts. Empathy helps individuals understand others' perspectives, enabling the discovery of common ground and mutually beneficial solutions. Additionally, empathy allows for a better understanding of the underlying reasons behind conflicts, leading to solutions that prioritize understanding, collaboration, and mutual respect, ultimately reducing tension in relationships.

In the realm of presales, empathy isn't just a skill; it's a critical behavior that supports successful client relationships and promotes personal and professional growth. It enables us to connect deeply with clients, understand their unique perspectives, and build trust through genuine engagement. By actively listening and adeptly interpreting verbal and non-verbal cues, we nurture meaningful conversations that lead to strong relationships and effective problem-solving. This empathetic approach diffuses tensions and allows us to navigate challenges skillfully, forging collaborative solutions that resonate with our client's needs and aspirations. Ultimately, empathy in presales creates an environment where mutual respect and understanding drive successful partnerships, sustainable business growth, and professional success.

Empathy and Diversity

For presales professionals, empathy and diversity are crucial for innovative problem-solving through varied perspectives. Leaders benefit greatly from assembling teams with diverse backgrounds and experiences, enhancing their ability to identify creative and innovative solutions for customers. Recognizing the value of empathy and diversity is essential for navigating challenges effectively in leadership roles, yet these principles are universally beneficial for fostering inclusive and innovative environments.

Understanding Different Perspectives

Individuals from diverse backgrounds bring viewpoints shaped by their experiences, beliefs, and cultural heritage, enriching the collective pool of perspectives within teams and organizations. Recognizing and valuing these diverse perspectives creates an inclusive and dynamic work environment where everyone feels respected and empowered to contribute. By actively listening to others' stories and viewpoints, we gain valuable insights into their backgrounds, challenges, and aspirations, strengthening relationships and broadening our understanding of the world. This empathetic approach encourages open-mindedness, constructive dialogue, and mutual respect, creating opportunities for learning and growth. Embracing and celebrating diversity enhances team cohesion, creativity, and innovation, driving success in the dynamic world of presales.

Insight Into Biases

Personal biases and prejudices, often operating unconsciously, shape our perceptions and interactions based on our experiences, cultural backgrounds, and societal influences. These biases can lead to unintentional discrimination and unfair treatment, affecting how we perceive and interpret others' actions. Recognizing and acknowledging these biases is the first step toward inclusive interactions and decision-making processes. By practicing empathy and seeking to understand others' experiences and perspectives, we can counteract biases, promote fairness, and cultivate compassionate and inclusive relationships. This involves listening with an open mind, suspending judgment, and considering others' feelings with respect, ultimately challenging stereotypes and bridging divides.

Awareness of Cultural Differences

Cultural differences encompass various elements such as language, customs, values, and social norms, all rooted in diverse histories and experiences. By acknowledging and honoring these differences, we create deeper understanding and appreciation for the diversity of human perspectives. Adapting to cultural nuances is crucial for effective communication and collaboration across boundaries, leading to mutual respect and harmony. Seeking to learn about different cultures expands our awareness, challenges biases, and enriches our understanding of global diversity.

Building Inclusive Environments

Building an inclusive organizational culture is crucial for creating unity and belonging among all individuals, regardless of their backgrounds or identities. This requires actively celebrating diversity and valuing each person's unique perspectives and contributions. Addressing barriers that marginalize certain groups, such as discrimination based on race, gender, ethnicity, sexual orientation, age, or disability, is essential for promoting equity, inclusivity, and belonging. Promoting diversity in leadership roles ensures that diverse voices contribute to innovation. Encouraging open dialogue and collaboration among diverse teams builds empathy, breaks down stereotypes, and enhances mutual respect. Organizations can boost employee engagement, productivity, and overall well-being by cultivating a sense of belonging and empowerment, driving sustainable growth and success.

I've personally benefited from building diverse teams. What I found was our differences became a tremendous strength for the team. We truly listened to each other and appreciated the varied perspectives brought to the group from our different backgrounds and experiences. I will share that there was a common characteristic I hired for when building the team: they were all friendly humans.

Story Time: Calling His Baby Ugly

During my time as a consultant, I would get assigned to help troubleshoot software systems for our clients. I was an experienced developer familiar with coding applications for local systems and the web.

We had a project for a refinery in Big Spring, Texas. They needed to retire an application that ran on a version of Microsoft Windows no longer supported. Due to their internal policies, this mission-critical application required an upgrade or replacement. I joined the project to understand the effort required to create a new application and to recommend how to move forward.

We were on a tight timeline, so I brought along an additional developer to assist me. Let's call him Steve. Steve was a good developer but was new to consulting. I had worked with him on a few previous projects and been pleased with his work, but I had always handled the client-facing tasks.

Big Spring is out in west Texas. To get to the refinery, we flew into Midland, Texas, then drove back east for an hour. Yes, Texas is big, and that was the most efficient way to get there. Driving straight from Dallas-Fort Worth would have taken about four and a half hours.

We flew in early on a Wednesday morning, and after the drive, we arrived at the refinery around 9 a.m. As this was an active plant, there was a check-in process and safety procedures to review. We met up with the local team responsible for the application at 10 a.m. and started getting oriented to the application. I'll never forget this one local guy, Bill, who seemed hostile to us from the beginning.

We took a lunch break and then resumed the review, working until just after 6 p.m. By this point, Steve and I had gathered the information we needed and wanted to spend time back at the hotel putting our recommendation together to present the next day. Our review process involved documenting the required functions to replicate and identifying any current bugs or errors. We found a few of those and some inefficiently implemented code. After wrapping up our presentation, we found a local pizza place for dinner.

Check-in didn't take as long the following day since we didn't have to repeat the safety briefing. We got into the conference room and waited for the local team to join us to review our findings. Bill was there and again seemed to be on edge.

I had decided to task Steve with leading the review of our findings. I saw this as a chance for him to take charge of the project if they accepted our proposal, and I wanted him to establish rapport with the refinery team. Of course, Steve was nervous as he opened the presentation and started working through what we had found. I was sitting towards the back, encouraging Steve as he presented and trying to read the rest of the room.

The first part of the presentation covered the critical functions, and we received positive feedback on our understanding of the application. The next section started getting into the bugs and errors, and that's when I noticed Bill starting to get red. It was obvious he was upset and getting more so by the minute. He wasn't saying anything or making any noise, but you could tell from his body language that he was about ready to explode.

Have you ever been in a meeting where something like that was going on with someone? I was getting a little concerned.

We hit a point in the presentation that felt like a good time for a break. I wanted to figure out what was going on with Bill. I motioned for Steve's attention, and when he acknowledged me, I suggested a 10-minute break.

Steve and I asked the local team lead for a minute of his time. We stepped away from the conference room, and I shared with him what I had observed with Bill. I asked if he had any thoughts on what was going on. He told us that Bill had written the application we were evaluating. I was stunned that we had not been given this information earlier and had not figured it out. It was a complete miss on my part, and it thoroughly explained Bill's reactions. We were calling his baby ugly.

Whenever you are faced with this type of project, whether updating some existing code or writing an entirely new application, it's a huge benefit to have a subject matter expert on hand.

Bill needed to be our subject matter expert for this, but we had just spent a couple of hours finding fault with what he had created, likely causing some ill feelings toward us. But really, could you blame him? Here were a couple of "city slickers" poking holes in something he had poured his blood, sweat, and tears into creating. This system had served the refinery well for five years, and the only reason it needed replacement was the outdated operating system.

We wrapped up the meeting with our recommendation to create a new application. We proposed a team of consultants, with Steve as the lead on the project working locally and me providing support remotely from our office in Irving, Texas. The team was happy with our approach and recommendation, and even Bill indicated he thought we had the right approach.

I suggested we take the team out for dinner before our flight (and drive) back. We ended up at a local diner where everyone knew everyone else. We had eight of us around a large table, and in no time, people were laughing and getting to know each other. I made sure Steve and I were seated close to Bill, and we intentionally asked him about his application. How did he get involved in building it? What was his toughest challenge? We got him to tell stories, and as we listened, we could see how proud he was of what he had created.

The change in Bill's attitude was surprisingly quick. When he realized that we understood his struggles and empathized with his sense of helplessness regarding the operating system requirement, he recognized our genuine concern for his situation. He no longer saw Steve and me as interlopers destroying something he created. He saw us as helpers who understood his perspective.

This encounter taught me a lot about empathy's critical role when working with others. It also taught me the importance of knowing the people in the room and their relationship to the project. I'm happy to report that this was a very successful project. Steve spent the next six weeks working at the refinery on creating and installing the new application. He and Bill ended up having a great working relationship, and Bill's insight and guidance were crucial in completing the project on time.

There is one last part to this story, but it doesn't illustrate any lesson learned. It's just a funny part of the dinner that brought some levity to a couple of intense days.

Evidently, the diner didn't always do the best job of cleaning their ice maker. Bill had ordered a glass of sweet tea—it's Texas, after all. Toward the end of dinner, Bill had a massive coughing fit and just about fell out of his chair. The entire diner was stunned into silence as no one was sure what was happening. Was he choking? Should we do something?

With all eyes on him, Bill spits out a moth frozen into an ice cube in his tea.

Now, since this is out in Big Spring, Texas, there's a beat of silence, and then everyone goes back to what they were doing before this happened, including eating their diner food and drinking their sweet tea. I'm unsure whether this was a regular occurrence, but it didn't seem too concerning to anyone else. It is sad that no one showed any empathy for the moth.

Notes

Suggestions to Develop Your Empathy

As we've learned, empathy is all about your ability to imagine another person's perspective or "walk a mile in their moccasins." It's challenging to set aside your values, beliefs, and judgment to do this, but it's a worthwhile skill to develop. Here are some activities you can engage in to practice and hone your empathy.

Work With a Trusted Colleague and Put Yourself in Their Shoes

The critical part here is a "trusted" colleague. This should not be someone in your management line but more of a peer, preferably from a different department or team. It's better if this person has a different background and experience from you. Those differences can be instrumental in making this an engaging activity.

- Arrange a one-on-one meeting with your colleague to discuss their background, experiences, and perspectives.
- Practice active listening during the conversation, focusing on understanding their viewpoint without judgment or interruption.
- Ask open-ended questions to encourage your colleague to share their thoughts, feelings, and experiences more freely.
- Engage in role-playing exercises, where you assume the role of your colleague and imagine how they might navigate various scenarios.
- Reflect on the similarities and differences between your own experiences and your colleague's, seeking to understand the factors that shape their perspective.
- Explore potential challenges or biases your colleague may face daily, and brainstorm ways to offer support or understanding.

- Consider how you can incorporate your newfound insights into your interactions with colleagues and others in your professional environment.
- Follow up with your colleague periodically to continue the dialogue and deepen your understanding of their perspective over time.

Look for Volunteer Opportunities in Diverse Communities

One of the best ways to understand someone else's perspective is to serve them. I enjoy volunteer opportunities, and I never fail to get more out of them than what I put into them. It doesn't matter how simple or complex the task is. The act of serving others will present you with learning and growth opportunities.

- Research volunteer opportunities in communities different from yours, focusing on causes or organizations that serve diverse populations.
- Contact the organization or community leader to express your interest in volunteering and inquire about their current needs.
- Attend volunteer orientation sessions or training workshops to familiarize yourself with the organization's mission, values, and guidelines for interacting with the community.
- Engage directly with the individuals you are serving, listening to their stories, experiences, and perspectives.
- Participate in activities or projects alongside community members, allowing you to observe their daily lives and challenges firsthand.

- Reflect on what you have learned from your interactions with the community, considering how their experiences and perspectives differ from your own.
- Identify common themes or insights that emerge from listening to the stories and perspectives of community members, and contemplate how these insights can inform your understanding of diversity and empathy.
- Share your experiences and insights with others in your social circle or professional network, raising awareness about the importance of volunteering in diverse communities and promoting empathy and understanding across different groups.

Notes

> "A conversation is a dialogue, not a monologue. That's why there are so few good conversations: due to scarcity, two intelligent talkers seldom meet."
>
> – Truman Capote

Chapter 5 – Have a Conversation

I'll admit that I haven't always been the best conversationalist. Developing this skill has been a continual journey throughout my career. It's never been about lacking things to say—I've always had plenty of thoughts to share. The challenge was mastering the art of conversation—actively listening and genuinely caring about what the other person had to say. As I've grown more comfortable with this behavior, I've been amazed at how many situations hinge on simply having a meaningful conversation.

This chapter is structured slightly differently from the others as I want to delve deeper into what I mean by the Timeless Behavior of **"Have a Conversation."** Instead of identifying the benefits delivered in their own section, I will weave them into the discussion. I'll also address common communication barriers we face in our roles and conclude with techniques to enhance your conversational skills in meetings and presentations.

The Art of Conversing

One of the earliest lessons I learned as a new presales professional was that my job wasn't to teach my audience how to use the software but to sell it. While I knew how to explain technical concepts, learning to sell and persuade took time. Throughout my career, I've discovered the immense value of honing the art of conversation.

One-way Versus Two-way Communication

If you run a training class, one-way communication may be the proper technique. You need to convey information to the audience, and they need to understand and internalize it. However, when you meet with prospects and present your solution or perform discovery on a business challenge they have, one-way communication won't help. In this situation, you need to have an old-fashioned conversation.

A good mental model to remember for conversing is one-way communication versus two-way communication. Are you talking more than the audience? If that's the case, you have likely slipped into instructing mode like I used to. Your focus has moved from learning about your audience to showing your solution. Is your audience talking more than you? In that case, you may not provide enough direction for the conversation and are missing an opportunity to learn. In a good old-fashioned conversation, both sides should be about equal in the amount of time spent sharing.

When that equal sharing happens in a conversation, you are no longer talking at someone but talking with someone. You actively listen to them and then share back based on what you've heard and learned. What does talking at someone sound like?

If you've been around as long as I have, you might remember the Peanuts cartoons from the late 1960s. If not, a quick search will show you. Whenever an adult spoke in those cartoons, it sounded like "wah wah wah, wah-wah." This clever technique showed how adults, often teachers, sounded to the kids. They created the sound with a muted trombone, but whether it's your voice or a trombone, you don't want to come across that way. You don't want to be talking at someone. You want your audience engaged and listening to you just as much as you are to them.

One-way communication limits the exchange of ideas between parties. When one person dominates the conversation without allowing room for input or feedback from others, valuable insights and perspectives remain untapped. This lack of exchange stifles creativity, hindering the potential for collaborative problem-solving and decision-making. In professional settings, such as meetings or negotiations, failure to facilitate a two-way exchange of ideas can lead to missed opportunities for exploring alternative solutions and reaching mutually beneficial outcomes.

When we are not conversing, the emphasis is often solely on delivering a message without regard for the recipient's thoughts, feelings, or concerns. This lack of empathy can result in a disconnect between the speaker and the audience, diminishing trust and rapport.

In **Chapter 4 – Show Empathy**, we learned that without acknowledging the perspectives and emotions of others, communication becomes transactional. Consequently, individuals may feel unheard, leading to decreased collaboration. Without investing in meaningful exchanges and shared experiences, relationships remain superficial and transactional, limiting the potential for growth, collaboration, and long-term success.

An Exchange of Information is Needed

When we apply the idea of having a conversation to our presales role, it's all about exchanging information with our audience. Both parties will bring valuable insights, context, and experiences.

This concept may seem obvious, but it's worth emphasizing: part of your job is to be the expert on your solution. As a technical specialist, you should thoroughly understand every aspect of your software and be able to provide specific examples of business problems it can solve, along with the benefits other companies have experienced. This crucial aspect of your role must be taken seriously. All the Timeless Behaviors in the world won't help you if you don't understand the solution you represent.

On the flip side, your prospect is the expert on their problem. While it may seem identical to issues faced by your other customers, it's essential to remember that this is their unique challenge and primary concern. Keep this in mind during discovery conversations or when presenting your solution. Examples from other customers can build confidence in your ability to help but always treat their problem as distinct and significant.

When learning about your prospect and their problem, it is crucial to create an environment where they feel safe sharing their thoughts and perspectives. Apply the techniques from Chapters 3 and 4 on active listening and empathy. These behaviors will create a safe space for open dialogue. The better you are at this, the more thorough your discovery will be and the stronger the relationship you'll build.

Use the knowledge you're gaining and your understanding of their business problem to ask questions that guide your audience toward the solution. Avoid treating discovery as an interrogation with a fixed list of questions. Instead, aim for an honest conversation, using open-ended questions to encourage dialogue and follow-up questions to explore deeper insights. Facilitating a great discussion and exchanging vital information will help you earn the status of a trusted advisor. This is a crucial step in convincing them that your solution will solve their problem and win their business.

Understand the Problem

I often refer to the job of presales as solving problems. The most critical step in solving problems is identifying and understanding them. I have countless stories where sellers felt confident a prospect needed our solution, but neither the seller nor the prospect contact could clearly describe the problem.

As a presales professional, the software you represent will have specific use cases that drive value for a company. One of the first steps in qualifying an opportunity is asking, "Does this company have a problem we can solve?" If the answer is no, move on to the next opportunity. If so, the next step is to understand their problem more deeply.

Through conversations with the prospect, determine the relative size of the problem. Size can mean many things, but one measure could be a financial impact. Consider this relative to the average cost of your software. If it's a $50,000 problem, they likely won't spend $500,000 to solve it. While calculating a "hard" return on investment (ROI) can be challenging with some solutions, businesses typically aim to lower costs, increase sales, or improve efficiency and quality. This ties back to Chapter 1 and the importance of business acumen in our presales roles.

Once we understand the size of the problem, we can work on the benefit of solving it. Companies aren't interested in just seeing your features and functions; they want to know how your solution helps them achieve their objectives. Some presales organizations have specialists who create value statements based on achieving specified outcomes. Even without this specialized role, presales professionals can use the problem's size and the desired outcomes to help prospects understand the benefits of solving the problem.

Equally important is understanding the risk to the organization if the problem isn't solved. These conversations can be tricky since they may impact people's reputations and careers, but highlighting that pain or risk can refocus the team on the importance of fixing the problem.

Whether discussing tough subjects like consequences or understanding the problem's size and scope, your ability to facilitate and drive a conversation can make or break your success in presales. It's worth investing time and effort into developing the behavior of conversing.

You are Selling a Solution, Not Training Your Audience on It

I began the chapter with this reminder, which bears repeating: I've seen too many software demonstrations turn into training sessions. As a presales professional, your role is to gain trusted advisor status and their business. This helps establish trust, positioning you as an advisor who wants to improve their company and working lives.

The product demonstration is just one piece of evidence at your disposal. You can also introduce case studies from other clients and share anecdotes about how similar companies addressed various issues. Audiences tend to enjoy these stories.

You can collaborate on the solution when you facilitate and drive the conversation with your prospect. If you engage in one-way dialogue, telling them what they need to do and how to do it, you miss the chance to have a conversation where they co-develop the solution with you.

There is tremendous benefit in mastering the art of conversation. As you've seen, this simple yet skillful behavior can be instrumental in your success. Digging deep in discovery to truly understand a prospect's business problem? It's just a conversation. Presenting a product demonstration? It's just a conversation with a prop.

Barriers to Conversing

It seems like such an easy idea—just have a conversation. The problem is that many barriers get in the way. Be aware of the different challenges that may impact your ability to practice the art of conversation.

Distractions and Lack of Attention

We don't hear too many stories about people sitting around with extra time on their hands. We're all busy, and something always clamors for our attention. With the number of people working from home, these distractions amplify as people often deal with sick children, deliveries, needy pets, or other everyday things that make it more challenging to focus and get work done. Holding someone's attention long enough for an honest conversation is a monumental ask.

When you can get time with someone, how do you know they are paying attention? Having cameras on during virtual meetings can help, but I'm sure we've all seen the person whose eyes are obviously looking at another monitor to the side or looking down, most likely at their phone. If people are not paying attention, they are not going to receive the information you are trying to share, and it's almost certain they won't be contributing to the conversation because they are not following it.

To make matters worse, we've developed all this wonderful notification technology for our computers and our phones. **Ding!** Your aunt Martha just posted a picture of the sourdough bread she baked from a starter that's 120 year old. **Ding!** Some random Business Development Representative just emailed hoping this message finds you well and are you looking to outsource your support tickets. **Ding!** A solicitor is ringing your doorbell even though you clearly have a "no soliciting" sign next to the buzzer.

Many people today feel overloaded and stressed about their work environments. Because of this, they may feel like meeting with you is a waste of their time. They may completely tune out and refrain from participating in the conversation. It's your job to find ways to engage with and get them involved. It's essential to get people to contribute and share their insights. Continue reading, and after the next Story Time, I'll outline some techniques you can use to engage your audience in the conversation.

Making Assumptions

While the responsibility for paying attention rests mainly with the audience, you must avoid making assumptions. Assuming intention can be a significant barrier to effective conversation. We risk misunderstanding the true meaning of someone's words or actions when we presume to know the motives behind them without seeking clarification. This can lead to miscommunication and conflict, hindering the flow of dialogue. Instead, approaching conversations with an open mind and a willingness to explore differing perspectives can help overcome this barrier and facilitate constructive communication.

Along with avoiding making assumptions, be alert for judging based on bias or stereotypes. Preconceived notions about individuals or groups can cloud our judgment and color our interactions. By allowing bias to influence our perceptions, we may inadvertently dismiss valuable insights or overlook opportunities for meaningful engagement.

Lack of clarity is another barrier that can hinder effective communication. When messages are unclear or ambiguous, misunderstandings can arise, leading to confusion and frustration. Lean into the Timeless Behavior of Listen Actively to ensure understanding and seek clarification from others when necessary.

Poor Nonverbal Communication

Misinterpretation can significantly hinder effective conversation, particularly in nonverbal communication. Individuals may interpret gestures, facial expressions, and body language without clear verbal cues to guide them. However, people can misinterpret these nonverbal cues, leading to misunderstandings. To overcome this barrier, practice active listening and seek clarification when in doubt to ensure an accurate understanding of messages.

Lack of engagement via nonverbal communication can also impede the flow of conversation. When participants fail to convey interest or attentiveness through their nonverbal cues, it can signal disinterest or detachment, hindering meaningful interaction. To address this barrier, individuals should maintain eye contact, nod in acknowledgment, and use facial expressions and gestures to convey engagement and understanding. With virtual meetings, the difficulty is magnified as you may have a screen full of attendees, and the images are too small to read nonverbal cues easily.

The term "poker face" describes the ability to prevent emotions from showing on your face or through nonverbal cues. If you are playing poker and end up with a really good hand, you don't want to break out into a big smile and tip off the rest of the players. I do not have a good poker face. My emotions are usually quite apparent on my face. It's something I'm working on. Not controlling body language can pose a significant barrier to effective communication, as nonverbal cues often convey subtle messages that can influence interpretations. Unintentional gestures, facial expressions, or posture can inadvertently convey disinterest, defensiveness, or hostility, undermining communication effectiveness.

Finally, be aware of the cultural differences that may appear in nonverbal communication. People interpret gestures, expressions, and body language differently across cultures. What is considered acceptable or polite in one culture may be perceived differently in another, leading to misunderstandings.

Emotional Barriers

Consideration of the other person's emotional state is crucial in facilitating effective conversation, as emotions can significantly influence communication dynamics. When individuals are aware of their conversation partners' emotions, they can adapt their approach and language accordingly, showing empathy and understanding.

Defensive reactions can pose a significant obstacle to a productive conversation. They often arise in response to perceived threats or criticism. When individuals feel attacked or challenged, they may instinctively become defensive, hindering the exchange of ideas and perspectives.

Anxiety or stress can impair communication effectiveness by heightening an individual's emotional state, making it challenging for them to focus and share their thoughts clearly. In **Chapter 3 – Listen Actively**, we discussed listening to respond versus listening to understand. Be aware that someone's default setting when feeling overly emotional or defensive may be listening to respond. If this is the case, having a productive conversation is almost impossible.

Lack of trust can impede meaningful conversation by undermining the foundation of mutual respect essential for effective communication. When individuals lack trust in their conversation partners or the integrity of the communication process, they may second-guess intentions or question the validity of statements, leading to skepticism.

Language Barriers

There have been many times in my presales career where my audience didn't speak the same language as me. This situation introduces a whole new set of barriers you must overcome.

Lack of comprehension can pose a significant barrier to effective conversation, particularly when participants struggle to understand each other's language or communication style. When individuals encounter unfamiliar vocabulary, complex syntax, or cultural nuances in conversation, they may experience difficulty grasping the intended meaning, leading to confusion and misunderstanding. When speaking with audiences who don't share the same base language as you, be aware of using idioms, slang, or cultural references that may be unfamiliar to them.

Challenges in exchanging ideas can hinder productive conversation, particularly when participants encounter difficulty expressing their thoughts or opinions due to language barriers. When individuals struggle to articulate their ideas fluently or succinctly in a foreign language, they may feel inhibited or frustrated, limiting their ability to engage in the conversation actively. To facilitate the exchange of ideas, simplify complex concepts, use visual aids or analogies, and encourage interactive dialogue.

As we practice the art of conversation, it's evident that numerous barriers can hinder effective communication. From the constant distractions of modern life to the subtle complexities of nonverbal cues and emotional dynamics, these obstacles challenge our ability to engage meaningfully with others. However, by employing the behaviors we've discussed so far; being authentic, listening actively, and showing empathy, along with awareness and a willingness to embrace diverse perspectives, we can overcome these challenges and create meaningful interactions.

Chapter 5 – Have a Conversation

Story Time:
Presenting With a Translator

We had a big, important meeting with a pharmaceutical company based in Brazil. I was the Sales Engineer supporting the opportunity, and several people from the company were involved in our discovery and preparation for the final solution presentation.

About four weeks before the big meeting, we learned that most of our audience would be Brazilian employees and that we should conduct the meeting in Portuguese. I don't speak Portuguese. I speak English, Texan, and a tiny bit of Spanish.

We quickly landed on the idea of hiring a translator who would be on the call with me, translating what I was saying during the product demonstration. Stop and think about this for a minute. I would deliver a presentation of the solution in our software, relying on another person to translate what I was saying while clicking through the screens. I was anxious about how this was going to play out. As I started imagining how the meeting would go, I realized I would need to have distinct chunks of thoughts (and speech) and then pause while the translator did their thing.

I didn't want the first time the translator, and I worked together to be in front of the prospect, so I asked to have two pre-meetings with the translator. The first would be for us to get some familiarity with each other and for me to gauge how well this person would follow our solution. The second meeting would be a full-on dry run or dress rehearsal, allowing me to practice those chunks.

The translator was a lovely person named Fernanda, and we had a nice time learning about each other. We talked about our families, our jobs, and our hobbies and discovered that we both played soccer. She was a striker, and I was a keeper, but we got along anyway. As I started discussing our solution and getting into the presentation, Fernanda caught on quite quickly.

We scheduled the dry run for the following week, and it was a valuable exercise. Fernanda had some suggestions around phrasing that we incorporated, and I modified how I had chunked up my script. We left that meeting feeling well-prepared for the presentation.

On the day of the big meeting, we got everyone connected and had a local seller deliver the setup and context for the meeting in Portuguese. When they wrapped, it was time for me to deliver the solution presentation. I introduced Fernanda and me (in English) and briefly described how we would spend the next thirty minutes. Then I stopped talking, and Fernanda jumped in to share what I had just said to them but translated into Portuguese. Because we had spent time together and practiced, I realized when she had completed that chunk, and I moved on to the next portion of the script. We went back and forth in that method, not once speaking over each other.

Our technology worked perfectly, and the coordination between Fernanda and me was seamless. We received favorable feedback and were asked a couple of times how long we had worked together.

During the meeting, the audience stuck with Portuguese, but at the end, several of them broke into English to thank us and let us know they had enjoyed the presentation. I had worked with Fernanda to learn how to say thank you—"Obrigado." I'm sure my pronunciation wasn't perfect, but the team appreciated the effort.

I share this story as a few different examples of the power of having a conversation:

1. I had a conversation with my Sales Leadership, sharing my concerns about being successful in the meeting without having extra time to work with the translator. This extra time was an additional expense for us, but I was able to convince my leadership of its importance and the value this would drive.
2. I had a conversation with the translator to learn a little about her and so she could learn a little about me. These few hours of familiarity helped us appear as a synchronized team during the presentation.
3. By seamlessly working in a coordinated fashion, Fernanda and I had a conversation with the team at the pharmaceutical company and did a good enough job that they ended up becoming a customer.

Conversational Language Techniques

It should be obvious that the Timeless Behavior of **Have a Conversation** is another vital behavior to develop and practice. It yields many benefits that are helpful in the day-to-day work of a presales professional. Practicing the art of conversation comes in handy in almost every situation. The final section of this chapter provides some activities and resource suggestions to assist you in growing your conversational abilities. I also wanted to include some techniques you can focus on immediately.

Speak as You Would to Your Friends

Everyone has a little bit of imposter syndrome inside them. Some of us just bury it deeper than others. One situation where imposter syndrome appears is when we present to others. We desire to be seen as intelligent and capable, and we (subconsciously or not) worry about how our audience perceives us. This worry pushes us to speak in a way that probably isn't natural. We try to impress others with our vocabulary, diction, and mastery of the subject. This approach is unnecessary and, worse, it doesn't work.

Consider the following paragraph:

> *"Our cutting-edge software solution promises to revolutionize your sales team's efficiency by reclaiming valuable time previously lost in the labyrinth of content searching. With our state-of-the-art technology, your sellers will effortlessly navigate through an intuitive interface, swiftly accessing precisely the content they require, thus catapulting productivity to unprecedented heights."*

That sounds great, right? There is some nice marketing effort behind that impressive set of words. What's really bad is that I've heard presales people say something very close to that when presenting their solution.

Now consider this paragraph:

"Our software will give your sellers back some time because it will be easier for them to find the content they need."

Simple. There is no extra marketing fluff. Which one of the paragraphs would be more memorable for the audience? Which paragraph gives them a clear idea of the benefit the software provides?

One of the fastest ways to improve how you are conversing with your audience is to speak to them the same way you'd talk to your family or friends. It's a simple mental model to carry with you as you practice the behavior of having a conversation.

Eliminate Technical Jargon and Buzzwords

Since many presales professionals have roots in technical fields, the allure of using technical jargon and buzzwords can be tempting. However, succumbing to this temptation can lead us down a treacherous path. While adding some industry lingo and flashy terminology may seem like a shortcut to credibility, it often creates barriers between us and our audience. Instead of facilitating understanding, excessive jargon can leave potential clients feeling lost and disconnected from the true essence of our solutions.

Picture yourself listening to a presentation littered with constant acronyms and the latest technobabble—it's like navigating a labyrinth blindfolded.

Our job is to deliver comprehension. To do that, we must avoid linguistic obstacles and embrace clear, straightforward language. And when acronyms inevitably enter the conversation, spell them out for the audience, whether we assume they're familiar with them or not. By prioritizing simplicity over complexity, we demonstrate our expertise and earn the trust and respect of those we engage with. After all, our true mastery lies not in our ability to dazzle with technical jargon but in our knack for conveying complex ideas with clarity and precision.

Use Positive Phrasing

This next technique can be subtle, but it's about putting a positive spin on whatever comes up. Employing positive phrasing in our conversations is not just a matter of politeness; it's a strategic choice that can impact the outcomes of our interactions. When we frame our messages in a positive light, we create an atmosphere of optimism and possibility.

Whether pitching a product, negotiating a deal, or offering feedback, our language shapes perceptions and influences outcomes.

Consider hearing this objection when presenting your solution, *"We're concerned that your reporting options don't provide the level of customization we need for our specific business requirements."*

We want to address the concern but do so in a way that assumes the audience will move forward with your solution and receive the functionality they require. A response using positive phrasing may sound something like this:

"I understand the importance of having customizable reporting options tailored to your business needs. Our software's reporting feature is designed

with flexibility and customization in mind. While our out-of-the-box reporting templates offer a solid foundation, we also provide customization capabilities that allow you to tailor reports according to your specific metrics, KPIs, and formatting preferences. Our support team will assist you in configuring the reporting functionality to align with your business objectives."

The response addresses the concern and paints the future picture, assuming the audience has your solution in place. The suggestion that "the support team *will* assist them" in configuring the reports rather than "the support team *is available* to assist them" is a subtle adjustment that puts the audience in the proverbial driver's seat.

When was the last time you went shopping for a car? Do you remember how quickly the salesperson wanted to get you into the driver's seat for a test drive? They do that because it creates that sense of ownership of the car in you. Using positive phrasing can perform the same function when presenting to your audience.

Facilitate Collaboration with "We"

Facilitating collaboration through language is a powerful way to establish rapport and build a partnership with your audience. By consciously using "we" instead of "you," you're signaling to the audience that you're in this together, working towards a shared goal. This simple linguistic shift transforms the conversation from a one-sided interaction to a collaborative exchange of ideas. It communicates to your audience that you're not just a presenter but a teammate invested in their success. Whether answering questions, addressing concerns, or outlining solutions, incorporating "we" language reinforces the idea that you're actively engaged alongside your audience, ready to navigate challenges and achieve objectives together.

Consider a situation where a prospect manages product names from a few different sources. As they evaluate your solution, it becomes apparent that they need to identify one source of truth. During the meeting, a member of the audience raises this question:

"It sounds like we need to align on the system of record for our product names and then replicate to the others. How would we do that with your software?"

The **"You Language"** response may be something like:

"Well, you would start with the system that is the most accurate and then create the process to replicate the data to the other systems on a regular basis. How often are the product names updated?"

That's a perfectly acceptable answer that could lead to additional discovery.

The **"We Language"** response would be slightly different:

"We'd want to work together to identify the system with the most accurate and up-to-date product names, and then we'd put a process in place to update the other systems as necessary. How often are the product names updated?"

Can you hear the difference in the two responses? Does the "We Language" response infer more of a collaborative or team approach to the issue? It's a very simple change that can significantly impact your audience and how they think about you and your solution.

Clarify and Summarize Often

Clarifying and summarizing during conversations serve as bookends, anchoring the discussion and ensuring understanding. Presales professionals can maintain clarity and alignment with their audience by periodically restating key points and confirming comprehension. Summarizing at the end of a conversation section highlights the key takeaways, reinforcing understanding and paving the way for the next steps, framing the conversation, and guiding it towards meaningful outcomes.

In summary (see what I did there?), developing conversational language techniques is essential for anyone seeking to engage and persuade their audience effectively. Presales professionals will create more meaningful interactions by adopting a natural, straightforward communication style, eliminating technical jargon and buzzwords, employing positive phrasing, facilitating collaboration through inclusive language, and utilizing clarification and summarization techniques. These techniques not only enhance comprehension and trust but also contribute to building solid relationships with clients and prospects. As presales professionals continue to refine and apply these techniques in their day-to-day interactions, they will experience greater success in guiding prospects and driving growth.

Notes

Suggestions to Develop Your Conversational Style

You can engage in many activities that can help develop your ability to converse naturally and easily with people. The most helpful one is to engage others in conversation. The more you can do this, the easier it will become. I have some specific suggestions you may find helpful below:

Work on Projecting a Calm, Relaxed Manner

It is much easier to have a natural, relaxed conversation when calm and relaxed. It's vital to achieve a calm mental state. If you struggle with this, consider engaging in some of these activities:

1. **Visualize Peaceful Scenes**: Take a moment to engage in visualization exercises. Imagine yourself in a tranquil environment, using all your senses to create a vivid mental image that promotes relaxation.
2. **Engage in Deep Breathing Exercises**: Incorporate deep breathing exercises into your daily routine. Try techniques like diaphragmatic breathing or box breathing to calm your nervous system and reduce anxiety.
3. **Try Mindfulness Meditation**: Dedicate a few minutes each day to mindfulness meditation. Focus on your breath, body sensations, or a calming mantra to bring awareness to the present moment and reduce stress.

Practice Speaking Plainly (and Cleanly)

Practice is critical when working on this behavior. Here are some suggestions for practicing.

1. **Record Yourself Speaking**: Record yourself speaking in various settings, such as presentations or conversations. Listen to the recordings and evaluate your speech patterns, clarity, and use of language. Identify areas for improvement and work on refining your communication skills.
2. **Use Everyday Language**: Consciously use everyday language that is easily understood by a broad audience. Avoid using specialized terminology or industry-specific jargon unless necessary, and opt for common words and phrases instead.
3. **Simplify Your Sentences**: Embrace the principle of simplicity in your communication. Strive to convey your message using the fewest words possible while maintaining clarity and precision. Practice simplifying your language without sacrificing meaning or depth.
4. **Pause and Reflect**: Incorporate pauses into your speech to allow yourself time to collect your thoughts and ensure clarity. Use pauses strategically to emphasize key points and give your audience time to digest information. This can be a great time to summarize.

Create a Library of Questions to Drive Conversations

Having a few questions in your back pocket can be helpful when you need a conversation starter. Remember that everyone's favorite subject is themselves, so ask a question that allows them to share something. Here are some examples:

1. **What do you do when you aren't working?**
   This gives the person a chance to discuss their hobbies and passions. Remember to listen actively when they respond.

2. **Where is your favorite place to visit?**
   This allows the person to share about a place they've lived or visited. Remember to focus on them and to give them your attention when they respond.
3. **What are you reading or listening to right now?**
   This allows the person to share a book or musical artist they enjoy. Remember to share appropriate non-verbal cues as they respond.

Endless questions like these can kick off a conversation with another person. Try to avoid questions that make assumptions about them, such as their marital status or whether they have children. Questions like those can be too personal and could potentially delve into an area of conflict in that person's life.

Notes

> "Humility means accepting reality with no attempt to outsmart it."
>
> – David Richo

Chapter 6 – Practice Humility

There's a musical artist from the 1970s and 80s named Mac Davis. Look him up when you get a chance. He had a song that came out in 1980 that I fell in love with instantly. It was titled "It's Hard to be Humble." Here's a sample of the lyrics:

> *Oh Lord it's hard to be humble*
> *When you're perfect in every way*
> *I can't wait to look in the mirror*
> *Cause I get better looking each day*
> *To know me is to love me*

> *I must be a hell of a man*
> *Oh Lord It's hard to be humble,*
> *But I'm doing the best that I can*

Source: LyricFind
Songwriters: Mac Davis
It's Hard to Be Humble lyrics
© Reservoir Media Management, Inc

I'm a bit embarrassed to admit that those lyrics could describe how I used to think about myself early in my career. Well, not the part about getting better-looking. I knew I was intelligent. Most answers came easily, and I quickly devised solutions to problems. The main issue was my eagerness to let everyone know about my brilliance. Learning the importance of humility and practicing humility took me a while.

What Does it Mean to Be Humble?

While preparing to write this book, I sought quotes to illustrate and document the behaviors, and I came across the one above by David Richo. Dr. Richo, PhD, MFT, is a psychotherapist, teacher, workshop leader, and writer based in Santa Barbara and San Francisco, California. He has authored several books on integrating the psychological and spiritual. This particular quote is from his 2008 book, "The Five Things We Cannot Change: And the Happiness We Find by Embracing Them."

Maintaining a Grounded Perspective

David Richo's quote encapsulates the idea of humility as accepting ourselves for who we are based on a true, authentic, and grounded perspective. The first Timeless Behavior, **"Be Authentic,"** focuses on aligning our actions with our values. The Timeless Behavior of **Practice Humility** goes a step further, emphasizing acceptance of our true selves.

Consider the distinction: being authentic means our actions reflect our internal values while practicing humility involves acknowledging and accepting our authentic selves. It's profound, isn't it?

Acknowledgement of Strengths and Weaknesses

One of the most challenging interview questions is, "What would you consider one of your weaknesses?" A person lacking humility might claim they have none, but that's not the response interviewers are looking for.

Someone practicing humility will likely provide a thoughtful answer, such as mentioning the need for better time management or the tendency to take on too many projects. The specific weakness is less critical than the admission itself; acknowledging a weakness shows self-awareness and humility.

We are generally good at recognizing and sharing our strengths. We might even identify areas for improvement, but a humble person accepts their faults and weaknesses, which isn't easy for the ego to digest.

Humility requires accepting that we cannot excel in every area. Instead of striving for perfection, we should acknowledge and embrace our imperfections. When we do so, we demonstrate humility and openness, creating growth opportunities. This acceptance involves setting aside ego, knowing when to seek assistance, and delegating tasks appropriately.

Putting Others First

When coaching new team members on practicing humility, I distill it into four simple words: "It's not about you." This straightforward concept serves as a guiding principle for developing humility. By shifting your focus from yourself to others, you can make significant strides in embodying this Timeless Behavior.

The second and third timeless behaviors, **Listen Actively** and **Show Empathy**, are crucial when you want to demonstrate that someone else is your primary focus. You've already learned about these behaviors, so now it's time to put them into practice. Listen actively during interactions and show genuine empathy towards others.

Putting others first also involves selflessly offering support, assistance, or resources without expecting anything in return. It's about genuinely caring for the well-being and success of others, whether by lending a helping hand, providing guidance, or offering growth opportunities without seeking reciprocity.

Elevating others is one of the most direct ways to put them first. Elevating others means actively supporting, empowering, and promoting the growth and success of those around us. Celebrate the achievements and contributions of colleagues, peers, and team members, and advocate for their advancement and recognition. This practice strengthens relationships, builds trust, and creates a sense of camaraderie and collective achievement within teams and organizations.

Being Curious About Others

Curiosity about others starts with showing genuine interest in their lives, experiences, and perspectives. This involves actively listening, asking thoughtful questions, and sincerely wanting to understand them better.

Understanding people better requires us to learn about them. Whether through conversations, shared experiences, or active observation, there is always something new to discover. By taking the time to learn about their backgrounds, interests, and beliefs, we gain valuable insights that help us navigate diverse environments with empathy and understanding.

Being curious about others also means actively engaging in conversations and interactions. It entails being fully present and attentive, participating in discussions, and contributing to the exchange of ideas. By engaging meaningfully, we show respect and appreciation for others' perspectives.

Curiosity encourages us to appreciate the diversity of human experience and embrace the richness of different cultures, backgrounds, and viewpoints. It involves recognizing and celebrating each individual's unique qualities and contributions, regardless of their differences.

Ultimately, curiosity about others is about building connections and meaningful relationships. It means seeking common ground, finding shared interests, and nurturing mutual understanding and trust. By approaching interactions with curiosity and an open mind, we create opportunities for connection and collaboration, enriching our personal and professional lives.

The Benefits of Being Humble

Now that we've spent some time on what it looks like to practice humility let's discuss the benefits of being humble:

Openness to Feedback

When we practice humility, we push our ego aside and open ourselves up for improved self-awareness. We can hear and accept critical feedback without going into defensive mode, which fosters enhanced performance as we learn and grow. We become more resilient as we accept our limitations and the knowledge that we don't have all the answers.

Committed to Continuous Learning

As humble humans who recognize they don't know everything, we experience personal growth and development as we explore new learning opportunities. This curiosity we develop will follow us through our careers and will drive fresh perspectives. As lifelong learners, we will be better equipped to navigate change and will experience expanded opportunities.

Building Authentic Relationships

The relationships we develop through humility will be stronger and deeper, based on honest communication and shared values. We will create trust and rapport faster in our relationships, and we will have mutual accountability in our network.

Perceived as Reliable and Trustworthy

Through our consistency, others will see us as reliable and trustworthy. We will be transparent in our dealings with others, and they will appreciate our sincerity and discretion.

Being a Collaborative Team Member

We will be sought-after team members who are valued for our support and encouragement of others. We prioritize flexible teamwork, embracing shared responsibility, and building consensus to achieve our common goals.

Practicing humility brings several benefits that ripple through our personal and professional lives. By having an open mindset and being receptive to feedback, we cultivate self-awareness and resilience, enhancing our capacity for growth. Through authentic connections built on trust and mutual accountability, we establish ourselves as reliable and trustworthy individuals, valued for our sincerity and discretion. As collaborative team members, we contribute to effective teamwork, prioritizing support, flexibility, and consensus-building to achieve shared goals.

The Opposite of Humility

When exploring behaviors, it's often helpful to consider their opposites. In the context of humility, several contrasting traits can emerge, each with detrimental effects in a presales environment. Let's examine a few of these traits.

Arrogance

Arrogance manifests as an air of superiority and disregard for others. An arrogant person prioritizes their agenda and tries to bully others into their way of thinking.

In a presales environment, arrogance shows when professionals dominate conversations, focusing more on their points than on understanding the audience's perspective. This hinders relationship building and the ability to become trusted advisors.

Many talented presales professionals come from technical backgrounds, where arrogance can be a common pitfall. However, humble presales professionals confidently set aside their egos to prioritize others.

Pride

Pride involves self-importance and taking excessive pleasure in one's accomplishments. A prideful individual is often closed-minded to ideas that might diminish their sense of importance.

For a presales professional, pride can lead to resistance against feedback or improvement suggestions from colleagues or clients. This reluctance to accept constructive criticism can stunt personal growth and damage client relationships, making it hard to succeed in a presales role.

While it's easy to become engrossed in personal achievements, it's problematic when these achievements close our eyes to growth opportunities. A humble presales professional acknowledges limitations and views constructive feedback as a professional development opportunity.

Ego

The ego represents our self-identity and source of self-esteem. When uncontrolled, it can dominate interactions and cause us to reject other perspectives.

An egocentric presales professional often focuses on their performance during meetings, neglecting their primary duty to engage and educate the audience. This self-focus can lead to audience disengagement.

Performance is an exciting part of the presales role, especially flawlessly executing a complex software demonstration. However, problems arise when the focus shifts from helping the audience understand the solution's value to simply showcasing the performance. A humble presales professional maintains a balanced ego, performing their tasks effectively while prioritizing the audience's needs and interests.

Narcissism

Narcissism is characterized by an excessive need for admiration and validation, often overshadowing genuine concern for others.

In presales, a narcissistic professional may spend excessive time establishing their credentials and highlighting their achievements. During software demonstrations, they emphasize the complexity of their setup rather than how the solution benefits the prospect.

The audience is there to find solutions to their business problems, not to be impressed by the presenter's self-promotion or clever setups. A humble presales professional allows their work to speak for itself and concentrates on delivering value to the client.

Self-Centeredness

Self-centeredness involves prioritizing one's own needs and agendas above those of others, often leading to a lack of empathy and understanding.

In a presales environment, a self-centered professional might rigidly adhere to their own meeting agenda, disregarding the client's specific needs and concerns. This approach can make the audience feel overlooked and unimportant.

This can be a tricky one, as most good presales professionals like to be prepared and usually create an agenda for how they want the presentation to go. Effective presales professionals are adaptable and ready to pivot their presentation to better address the audience's immediate concerns. A humble presales professional recognizes that their primary goal is to facilitate understanding and alignment, focusing on the audience's needs above their own.

In summary, a lack of humility in a presales environment can lead to negative traits such as arrogance, pride, egocentricity, narcissism, and self-centeredness. These behaviors can impede effective communication, damage client relationships, and distract from the primary goal of addressing the audience's needs and demonstrating the solution's value. Conversely, a humble presales professional prioritizes others, setting aside ego and personal agendas to build meaningful connections. Therefore, practicing humility is essential for success in presales.

Chapter 6 – Practice Humility

Story Time:
A Humble Presales Professional

Don't worry. It's not a story about me! That wouldn't be very humble, would it?

I joined a company just in time for their annual Sales Kickoff (SKO) a few years back. For those unfamiliar, SKOs are events where the entire go-to-market team gathers, usually at the start of the year, to align on upcoming goals. Before the pandemic, these were always in-person events.

My official start date was January 17th, right after the SKO. Not wanting to miss the chance to meet my future colleagues, I took some vacation time from my current job and made plans to attend.

During the interview process, I met several people, and knowing I would join them at the SKO, I reached out to a few to make plans to connect. One of them was James Brentano.

The SKO was in Las Vegas. James had arrived earlier in the day, and we made plans to meet for dinner after I landed. We met in the bar at the hotel where we were staying. Over the following years, there would be many times when James and I and others from our team would share drinks and stories.

A Friendly Human in Presales

James was friendly and welcoming. We quickly started sharing stories about our lives and careers. He had been in presales longer than I had and enjoyed his current role as an individual contributor. When I mentioned my experience and IBM's leadership training program, James said, "Oh, you must be the person who will replace Brian."

I found this funny since I hadn't officially joined the company yet, and there was no plan, to my knowledge, for a leadership change. I asked James why it wouldn't be him. It was clear he was highly skilled and more than qualified. He told me he had been a leader before but was happy and content being responsible only for himself at this point in his career.

His comment turned out to be prophetic. By December of that year, our manager, Brian, took on a new role in sales, and I had the opportunity to lead the team.

Let's pause here to highlight James' humble behaviors. He was comfortable with his abilities and didn't need to flaunt his accomplishments. He understood his value to the organization and was content in his role. He was also an excellent presales professional; all the sellers wanted to work with him.

When I became the Sales Engineering leader, James continued to be an invaluable resource for me and the team. We added team members without presales experience and trained them to be skilled professionals. James always shared his knowledge and was incredibly patient in teaching. Not all highly skilled technical people possess such patience, further showcasing James' humility. He put others first, helping his teammates develop their abilities.

Our company was acquired a few years later, and I took on a new role leading a different team. I convinced James to join me, where he continued mentoring and coaching our junior colleagues.

Having James in my corner was a huge benefit. I had someone to share ideas with who had similar experience and expertise. I considered him a partner in leading the team and will always be grateful for our time working together. To this day, James and I text and talk regularly, checking in on each other's lives and families.

I have stories about other presales professionals who lacked humility. Where do you think I got the list of all the bad behaviors? We'll leave them unmentioned for now, but if we ever chat in person, just ask, and I might spill the beans on a few.

Notes

Suggestions to Develop Your Humility

The most effective way to work on humility is to model humble behaviors and review the negative behaviors listed earlier in the chapter. Self-awareness will be key as you continue your journey of growth and development. Here are some additional activities you can consider:

Look for Opportunities to Serve Others

One of the best ways to learn about humility is to put others first by serving them. Check around your workplace or community for opportunities to serve. Many organizations have programs that allow interested individuals to participate in various ways.

- Contact local charitable organizations about volunteering.
- Check with Schools or Churches about service projects, mentoring, or coaching.
- Ask if you can be of service to your team or other departments at work

When serving others, focus on the act of service. Don't enter it with the expectation of receiving something in return.

Practice Graciousness in Your Successes

You are indeed responsible for your success, and you should be proud of what you have accomplished. But have you considered how many others have contributed to your development and growth? Your successes are also their successes.

1. Reflect on the people who have helped you along your career journey. (parents, family, teachers, coaches, colleagues, mentors)

2. Make a list of those people and how they helped you. Be as specific as you can be.
3. Consider writing a letter to one (or more) of those individuals or making a social media post thanking them for contributing to your success.
4. As part of your next success or achievement, look for ways to inspire or encourage someone else.

Going forward, make successes and achievements more about "we" than "me."

Find Ways to Elevate Others

Once we recognize and accept that our success is shared with everyone who has influenced and shaped us, we should find ways to elevate others. This is a call to action that you'll need to implement throughout your career, but here are some suggestions to get you thinking.

1. **Give Acknowledgement and Recognition**
   Be someone who recognizes the contributions of others in visible ways. This can be calling someone out in an email or on team calls. Done properly, this can boost morale.
2. **Provide Opportunities for Growth**
   Offer opportunities for skill development, learning experiences, and career advancement. This could involve recommending individuals for special projects or advocating for their participation in training programs.
3. **Share Knowledge and Expertise**
   Be like my friend, James. Share your knowledge, expertise, and resources with others. Offer to collaborate on projects, share best practices, or provide mentorship to help others improve their skills and achieve their goals.

Chapter 6 – Practice Humility

I'll close this chapter by providing two examples of this principle from my career.

The first example is the Associate Sales Engineer program I created with my friend and colleague, Warren Villanueva. This program elevates individuals with no prior presales experience and trains them to become excellent presales professionals. We actively sought out non-traditional presales talent to add to our team. As of May 2024, thirteen people have gone through our program in four and a half years, and those individuals consistently rank among the highest-performing sales engineers on the team. Developing this program has been incredibly fulfilling, and I enjoy seeing the program graduates succeed.

The second example is making time on my calendar for conversations with others. I'm always happy to speak with anyone interested in learning about presales. These people are often new to the profession and want to hear about my experience. At last count, I had just passed one hundred conversations. I feel like I get as much, if not more, from these chats as the other person.

A Friendly Human in Presales

Notes

> "We are, as a species, addicted to story.
> Even when the body goes to sleep,
> the mind stays up all night,
> telling itself stories."
> – Jonathan Gottschall

Chapter 7 – Tell a Story

The ability to tell a story well is vital for anyone whose job is to convey information. Humans are pre-wired to absorb and understand information shared in a story format. The problem comes when we ask a very simple question.

What is Storytelling?

You would expect a simple question to have an equally simple answer, but there are as many definitions of storytelling as storytellers. I'll share my definition of a story later in the chapter, but let's begin with a brief history of stories.

The Origin of Stories

Storytelling has been an integral part of human communication since ancient times, dating back to the dawn of civilization. It served as a vital tool for sharing crucial information about survival, such as identifying dangerous animals or edible plants. Cave paintings in France, estimated to be over 30,000 years old, provide evidence of early storytelling, offering glimpses into the narratives of our ancestors.

As history progressed, storytelling evolved alongside it, incorporating poems, songs, and oral traditions passed down through generations. However, it wasn't until around 3400 BC, when writing was invented in Mesopotamia, that stories began to be documented.

I like to cite the story of the tortoise and the hare as an example. No matter where I am in the world, I can show a visual of a rabbit and a turtle or just mention the story's title, and people will immediately know the story and its moral. The story is credited as one of Aesop's Fables. Aesop, a Greek storyteller who lived between 620 and 564 BC, collected and shared this and other stories. Despite its ancient origins, the moral of this fable remains universally recognized across cultures. Consider the power of storytelling—after nearly 2,700 years, "The Tortoise and the Hare" remains ingrained in our collective consciousness. Harnessing even a fraction of this narrative power can significantly enhance our effectiveness as presales professionals.

Storytelling remains a cornerstone of communication in our modern world. It still effectively passes information, knowledge, wisdom, values, and traditions from generation to generation. Whether gathered around the dinner table with family or chatting with friends, storytelling is integral to how we connect and bond—even when we've heard the stories countless times before. Even when meeting new acquaintances, we genuinely understand and appreciate each other through sharing personal narratives. We could read their resume or ask them for a biography, but where's the fun in that?

Stories have evolved from mechanisms for sharing critical information to become forms of entertainment that drive big business across various industries. In music, songs often tell stories of love, loss, and success, captivating audiences worldwide and generating revenue through album sales, streaming, and concerts. Books continue to captivate readers' imaginations, with bestsellers driving lucrative publishing deals and potential film adaptations. Theatrical plays transport audiences to different worlds, offering live storytelling experiences that engage and entertain. Television series and movies have become cultural phenomena, with streaming platforms and box office hits raking in billions annually.

Meanwhile, the video game industry has revolutionized storytelling, offering immersive narratives and interactive experiences that rival traditional media forms. The new virtual reality (VR) and augmented reality (AR) technologies are blurring the lines between fantasy and reality and providing a whole new immersive experience. In essence, stories have become a means of entertainment and a big part of the global economy.

From ancient cave paintings to modern multimedia platforms, storytelling has transcended time, evolving into a potent force that shapes cultures and economies worldwide. Its universal appeal entertains and drives significant economic activity, underscoring its enduring relevance and power.

Storytelling has (Too) Many Definitions

When I teased earlier in the chapter that you can get a different definition of storytelling from just about anyone you ask, I meant it in the specific context of presales. We all understand storytelling and recognize it when we experience it, but how would you explain to a presales professional how to tell a story during their presentation?

I've seen many attempts to explain or codify the process of telling a story. Some people will tell you that modern storytelling is just a formula you apply to the narrative you want to share. They believe you must follow their suggested structure to develop a compelling story to win over your audience.

The formula involves identifying the hero and the villain and then defining the hero's journey. Here's where he or she experiences the conflict, and then the magic twist happens, and the plot thickens. Plug tab A into Slot 4 while applying firm pressure and rotate slowly counter-clockwise. Develop the character to show growth and learning. Don't forget to highlight how the "before" situation was bad, and now the "after" is good. And no matter what, leave an opening for the sequel.

I think some IKEA assembly directions got mixed up, but honestly, I'm not sure. Much of the formulaic approach to storytelling seems far too complex to be useful in a presales environment. I believe there is a much simpler way to tell a story and convey the desired information to my audience.

My Definition of Storytelling

When I started thinking about using a storytelling approach to my presentations versus showing features and functions, I went back to the beginning. I thought a lot about what I wanted to accomplish when presenting a software solution to an audience. It became clear to me that the outcome I wanted to achieve was about passing along information and knowledge—the most basic tenets of what storytelling is all about. That put me on a clear path to remove unnecessary fluff and junk and focus on clear, simple ways to impart information to my audience.

I focused on speaking in plain language, stripping away complex technical jargon and buzzwords, opting instead for clear, straightforward language that anyone could understand. These are some of the conversation techniques we covered in **Chapter 5 – Have a Conversation**. This approach ensured that the audience remained fully engaged and could easily grasp the essence of the narrative. I tried to paint vivid mental images of the audience's potential future with the proposed solution in place, enabling them to envision the benefits and outcomes in a tangible way. This simplicity and clarity enhanced the impact of the narrative and facilitated a deeper understanding for the audience.

I didn't focus on constructing a hero's journey narrative, but I did prioritize personalizing the presentation whenever possible. This involved various strategies, such as featuring a member of the audience as a user in the system and offering a firsthand perspective of the solution. At other times, I tailored the demonstration by incorporating data relevant to a current project the audience was working on. I looked for ways to bring the company's branding into the demonstration environment by adding their logo or including their brand colors. These personal touches created audience touchpoints and helped make my presentation more memorable.

In crafting your story, you must give your audience a compelling reason to care by highlighting what's in it. Center your narrative around the outcomes your solution delivers: increasing revenue, decreasing costs, improving efficiency, or some variation thereof. By emphasizing these tangible benefits, you establish a reason for your audience to pay attention and invest their time in your presentation.

Finally, you should find ways of making your presentation interesting and fun. The techniques you use will depend on your authentic personality and style. You will need to experiment with different elements to learn what works best for you. Consider incorporating creative visual elements that convey information and spark curiosity and engagement. For example, you could use infographics, animations, or interactive charts to visualize data and statistics compellingly. Instead of overwhelming your audience with text-heavy slides, use images, icons, and symbols to convey key messages and concepts visually.

Let's assume you are presenting a marketing solution, and one of the benefits is giving back 5 hours a week to each seller as they can find the content they need faster. You know the company has 600 sellers, so simple math suggests a savings of 39,000 hours a quarter or 156,000 hours over an entire year. 156,000 sounds like a lot of time, but what would it look like? It's the equivalent of 17+ years. How could you represent that in an image?

In short, the definition of storytelling that I subscribe to involves using plain, non-technical language to convey the desired information to my audience. I look for ways of personalizing the presentation, including incorporating elements from their brand. I focus on the benefits my solution will provide to give them a reason to care about the presentation, and I look for ways to make it interesting and fun. That's the story I focus on crafting and sharing.

Storytelling Versus Showing Features and Functions

I mentioned how I changed how I presented from just showing features and functions, which is a common way for technical people to demonstrate. Our engineer brains like to know how things work and the names of the various product features. We want to share that knowledge with the audience, ensuring they see all those features and hear all those product names. Here's the thing, though. They don't care about any of that. They just want their problem solved.

In **Chapter 5 – Have a Conversation**, we discussed the difference between instructing someone on your solution versus convincing them that it is the best option. Falling into the feature/function trap is a lot like instructing. You've forgotten your true purpose in providing the demonstration—to convince your audience. When you are going through the features and functions of your solution, it's also likely that you are engaging in one-way communication versus two-way. You are no longer having a conversation. You are delivering a monologue.

When sharing stories, you aren't just delivering information but creating an emotional connection with your audience. By weaving narratives into your presentation, you capture their attention and draw them into the journey you're sharing. Instead of passively receiving facts and figures, they become active participants in your story, making the experience more memorable and creating a bigger impact.

Context is crucial for understanding and retention when sharing the values and benefits your solution delivers. Storytelling provides a powerful tool for offering this context by framing information within a narrative. Setting the scene and outlining the challenges give your audience a deeper understanding of the issues. This contextual richness enhances comprehension and enables your audience to see the relevance and significance of the information you present.

People connect with stories because they see themselves reflected in the characters and situations portrayed. When you use storytelling in your presentation, you make the content relatable to your audience's experience. You create a sense of empathy and understanding by sharing anecdotes or case studies that resonate with their lives.

Running through your software showing features and functions feels like training and only answers the question, "Do you understand what I just did?" When you focus solely on showcasing features and functions, you risk overwhelming your audience with technical details without providing context or relevance. While they may grasp the mechanics of what you're presenting, they might struggle to understand why it matters to them. This approach often leads to disengagement and a lack of buy-in, as the audience fails to see the value in what you're offering beyond its surface attributes.

Engaging the audience with storytelling and providing context answers the question, "Do you understand why I did what I just did?" Storytelling goes beyond the surface level of features and functions to explain their underlying rationale and significance. Instead of just demonstrating how a product works, you illustrate why it was developed in the first place and how it addresses real-world needs and challenges. By providing this context, you help your audience connect the dots and appreciate the relevance and value of what you present.

Storytelling Techniques

In this section, we'll explore various techniques to enrich your presentations as you embrace the art of storytelling. As you refine your skills, consider gradually integrating these elements, allowing yourself to grow and adapt. I encourage you to look for low-risk opportunities to experiment with some of these to see what works best for your individual style.

Have a Narrative

When I suggest having a narrative, I'm not talking about an overly formulaic hero journey with villains and a plot twist. I recommend crafting a cohesive story with specific characters and a clear beginning, middle, and end. Present the events in your story in a meaningful sequence, likely in chronological order.

For example, if you are demonstrating a solution for managing support tickets, your story should feature a person who submits a ticket and a person who manages the ticket. At the beginning of the story, the support ticket gets opened. The middle of the story covers managing the ticket, and the end of the story involves closing the support ticket. Yes, that's a simple example, but simple is good!

Remember that you are taking your audience on a journey with you. You are very familiar with the path—sometimes too familiar, but your audience is not. You are their guide, and you are responsible for making the path easy for them to follow.

Current State Versus Future State

Another helpful technique is to base your story around the current state of things for your audience versus the future state they will enjoy with your solution in place. This is all about creating a vision for them of how their daily work will be improved.

When describing the current state, avoid being too negative. Your audience will likely include people responsible for the current state, and you don't want to alienate them. Simply state the challenge that exists today. Referring to the support ticket example in the previous section, you might describe the current state:

"In our previous conversation, you all shared that your existing support ticket system is difficult for end users and doesn't provide the detailed reporting you need. Do I have that right?"

The future state is where they will be after implementing your solution. Use the positive phrasing discussed in **Chapter 5 – Have a Conversation** when describing the future state. Highlight the benefits and value they will realize and describe the outcome. Paint them a mental picture—put the audience in the driver's seat of that new car. With our support ticket example, your future state description may sound like:

"In the new system, your users will be able to submit a ticket with one click, and the reports you need will be right on your dashboard when you log in."

With a little bit of discovery ahead of your presentation, you will be able to craft a current-state versus future-state story easily and quickly. This can be a powerful way to keep the audience engaged during your presentation.

Personalize the Journey

A dependable way to engage your audience is to make it about them. Look for opportunities to personalize the story you are telling. As you go through your presentation, use the names of people in your audience. When setting up examples, use terminology and situations that are familiar to them. Make your solution look and feel like something they know.

Using our same support ticket example, determine the name of someone who would likely submit a support ticket. Find out who would manage and close the ticket. Use those names as you walk through the demonstration. When performing discovery, ask what type of support tickets are common and then use that as an example. It may sound something like this:

"Mary needs to submit a support ticket to request a license for Camtasia. With one click, she's already on the submit ticket screen, and her credentials are captured through Single Sign-On. She selects the requested type of software license and then chooses Camtasia. One more click, and the ticket is submitted. Mary, how would this new process benefit you?"

[Later on in the demonstration]

"Bob logs in and sees a new request from Mary. He clicks on the request and notices she is requesting a Camtasia license. Her department is authorized, and licenses are available for deployment. He creates the package and updates the ticket. Since no further approval is needed for this ticket type, he closes the ticket and notifies Mary via email. Bob can access the License Report from his Dashboard and see all users with a current Camtasia license, including Mary, who was just added. Bob, what additional value would that type of reporting provide to you?"

You can understand how this personalized story is more compelling to your audience than describing the fields and the clicks. Using personalization makes your solution relatable, relevant, and understandable.

Use Analogies and Anecdotes

Analogies can be incredibly effective in illustrating complex concepts. For instance, in a presales situation explaining the benefits of a cloud-based storage solution, you might use the analogy of a virtual filing cabinet. You could liken the cloud storage system to a modern, digitized version of a traditional filing cabinet, where files and documents are stored securely in a centralized location accessible from anywhere with an internet connection. This analogy helps to convey the idea of convenience, accessibility, and organization that the cloud storage solution offers.

On the other hand, anecdotes provide a personal touch and can help humanize your presentation. Let's say you're pitching customer relationship management (CRM) software to a sales team. You could share a brief anecdote about a previous client who struggled with managing customer data manually, leading to missed opportunities and lost revenue. By implementing the CRM software, the client could streamline their sales process, track interactions more efficiently, and ultimately increase their sales performance. This anecdote highlights the real-world impact of the solution and resonates with the audience by showcasing a relatable scenario and tangible results.

Creating vivid imagery is essential in engaging your audience and making your narrative come alive. Analogies and anecdotes play a crucial role in this aspect of storytelling by providing concrete examples and scenarios that the audience can easily visualize and relate to. When you describe the cloud-based storage solution as a virtual filing cabinet or recount the success story of a client who benefited from implementing CRM software, you're painting vivid mental pictures that help your audience understand the concepts in a tangible way.

Using shared experiences further enhances the effectiveness of analogies and anecdotes in storytelling. When you relate your examples to situations or challenges your audience members have likely encountered, you create a sense of connection. Whether you describe the frustration of managing overflowing file cabinets or recount the satisfaction of streamlining sales processes, shared experiences help bridge the gap between your message and your audience's reality.

Finally, incorporating analogies and anecdotes can significantly enhance retention. You create a memorable and impactful presentation by appealing to both the logical and emotional aspects of the audience's brain. When the audience can vividly recall the virtual filing cabinet analogy or the success story of the CRM implementation, they're more likely to retain the key messages and take action based on your presentation.

Consider Different Learning Styles

Having spent a few years as a software instructor, I delved into understanding various learning styles to excel in my role. It became evident that people absorb information differently—some are visual learners, some are auditory learners, and others are kinesthetic learners. What's fascinating is that engaging multiple learning styles can significantly enhance information retention.

Visual and auditory learning styles are often addressed naturally in presentations through slides and spoken words. However, catering to kinesthetic learners adds an extra layer of engagement. These individuals thrive on involvement and immersion. Incorporating storytelling that places them amid the action or using descriptive language to evoke sensations can effectively engage this learning style.

For instance, consider this scenario:

"Picture a crisp fall morning. You've just poured yourself a steaming cup of coffee, its rich aroma filling the air. As you settle into your desk and log in, a new email notification chimes, informing you that your boss has selected you to join a software selection committee."

By immersing kinesthetic learners in a sensory experience, you tap into their preferred learning mode and keep them actively engaged throughout your presentation.

But what about auditory learners? For them, it's all about the nuances of speech—the pace, tone, and inflection. Clear articulation, varied pitch, and controlled volume can make your presentation captivating for this group. Simply put, strive to be a compelling voice to listen to. And for visual learners, stay tuned for our discussion in the next section.

Remember, you won't always know your audience's learning styles. That's why it's prudent to assume a mix of all three types and incorporate techniques that cater to each, ensuring your presentation resonates with every attendee.

Incorporate Strong Visuals

Engaging visual learners is essential, but the impact of strong images extends beyond catering to a specific learning style. One significant benefit is the variety they bring to your presentation. We've all endured those dreaded 'death by PowerPoint' sessions, where slide after slide inundates us with dense text and monotone delivery. Yeah, don't do that.

I've also seen the opposite, where a presenter seems to be trying too hard and includes mismatched images in an attempt to create a visual story. Don't do that, either. An effective presentation seamlessly integrates slides with both text and visuals.

Here's a quick example from a presentation I've delivered on storytelling. The slide I show has an image of a cartoon rabbit next to an image of a cartoon turtle. No matter where I present this slide or the demographic of my audience, everyone makes the connection from the image to the story of the Tortoise and the Hare. Now, that's a powerful image!

When sourcing images, prioritize quality over quantity. Blurry or pixelated visuals distract your audience and diminish the perceived quality of your presentation and, consequently, your solution. Avoid using watermarked images or unauthorized content found online. Instead, leverage reputable sources like Unsplash.com, which offer high-quality, royalty-free images.

Before using images from a prospective buyer's website, take the time to ask for permission. There have been times when I contacted a company's marketing team, and they provided approved assets that I incorporated into my presentation.

Remember, strong visuals enhance your storytelling, while poor-quality images undermine it. Be thoughtful about including visuals that captivate your audience and reinforce your narrative, elevating the impact of your presentation.

Share Case Studies

Integrating case studies into your presentations will enhance your storytelling approach. Case studies ground abstract concepts in real-world scenarios, bringing realism to your presentation. By showcasing how your solution has been applied in actual situations, you provide concrete examples that resonate with your audience's experiences and challenges.

Case studies shed light on the challenges other companies encountered along the way. You demonstrate your problem-solving capabilities by candidly addressing obstacles your clients face and the solutions implemented to overcome them. This showcases your adaptability and resilience, reinforcing your audience's confidence in your ability to address their challenges effectively.

One of the primary functions of case studies is to demonstrate the success of implementing your solution. You provide evidence of your solution's effectiveness by presenting measurable outcomes, such as increased efficiency, cost savings, or improved performance.

In addition to showcasing the outcomes, case studies offer valuable insights into the process behind the success. Outlining the steps taken from problem identification to solution implementation provides a roadmap for your customer's journey.

By incorporating case studies into your presentations, you provide your audience with evidence that illustrates your solution's tangible benefits and practical applications. These real-world examples enhance your presentation's credibility and inspire confidence and trust in your ability to deliver results.

The Benefits of Storytelling

Storytelling is an age-old technique that humans are pre-wired to appreciate. It's a powerful and effective tool to incorporate into your presentations and provides several benefits.

Audience Engagement

You compete for your audience's attention with countless other priorities. Using storytelling keeps your audience interested and engaged in your presentation. The more we engage the audience, the better the chance they will receive our message and develop a relationship with us as their trusted advisor.

Emotional Connection

When companies evaluate software solutions, they will see multiple solution presentations. At the end of the day, people will buy from the team they like the best and trust the most. It is crucial for us as presales professionals to be able to create an emotional connection with our audiences. Effective storytelling is a reliable technique for making those connections.

Retention

When companies see multiple presentations, they receive a lot of information. You want them to remember what you shared with them about the benefits your solution provides and the outcomes they can achieve. If you can deliver this message through storytelling, you make it easier for them to retain it.

Differentiation

After seeing multiple software demonstrations, people are asked to decide which solution they prefer. I worried about my presentation looking and sounding like the others, and I wanted to come across as something different and memorable. Effective storytelling will differentiate your presentation from the others and make you memorable.

Storytelling offers several benefits for effective presentations. First, it enhances audience engagement by capturing their attention and fostering participation, increasing the likelihood of message reception. It facilitates the creation of emotional connections with the audience, which is crucial for building rapport and preference during competitive evaluations. Additionally, storytelling makes your message more memorable and impactful, ensuring key points about your solution's benefits and outcomes resonate long after the presentation. Finally, by employing storytelling effectively, you differentiate your presentation from others, leaving a lasting impression that sets you apart in the minds of your audience.

Story Time:
A Few Stories from Down Under

I was working in my home office one day when I received an email on which I was copied. In the email, my boss, Aaron Beazley, suggested to someone else that I could be in Australia the week after next for an important presentation. I thought it was funny that the email wasn't directed to me, asking about my availability. Still, I messaged Aaron to ask if this was a serious request and whether I needed to start making travel plans.

He assured me that it was a serious request. To make this part of the story shorter, I ended up traveling to Australia with Aaron to support an important software presentation. It was my first trip down under, and I returned with a few stories from the trip that people seemed to enjoy. Since this is the storytelling chapter, I thought I'd share a few here. I don't know that these stories illustrate any universal truths about presales or storytelling, but see what you think.

A Tale of Two Demonstration Scripts

The presentation we were going there to deliver was a Request for Proposal (RPF) response demonstration. The prospect had several vendors respond to the RFP and asked the down-selected vendors to present. They gave us two hundred and fifteen individual requirements to demonstrate. The prospect planned to score the vendors on each of these requirements. Delivering this type of demonstration is not fun.

As part of my preparation, I created a slide deck with each requirement numbered and detailed on a slide. My intent was to ensure the audience followed along, saw the software solution to each requirement, and scored us favorably. I finished up the deck and had my demonstration environment configured and ready to go.

As I reviewed the requirements and practiced my presentation, I realized that I could tell a more comprehensive story if I changed the order of the requirements. I created a second deck with the requirements still numbered and detailed but in my storytelling order. I shared this with Aaron, and we decided to ask them which method they preferred. I prepared to deliver either one for them.

On the day of the meeting, we began with introductions and the obligatory overview slides. (Are they really obligatory? But I digress.) When it was time for me to start the solution presentation, I explained to the audience that I had prepared a presentation addressing their requirements in the original order. While I was happy to present in that order, I believed it would be easier to follow the story if I arranged it differently. To my delight, they agreed with my proposed storytelling order!

I pulled up the first slide, reminded them of the requirement, and then switched over to the software to show the solution. When finished, I went back to the slide, checked for understanding, and suggested they take the time to score the requirement while the solution was fresh in their minds. After a few seconds, I repeated the process to the next slide and requirement.

It was about four hours of presenting with a couple of breaks, but we completed all two hundred and fifteen requirements in the allotted time. As we were wrapping up the meeting, the team told us how much they appreciated the approach of covering the requirements in a different order. They shared that it made more sense and was a better story. But the best compliment was when they told us that putting their requirements in a story order proved how well we understood their problem. They also shared that NO OTHER VENDOR did that.

Music Trivia Wins the Day (and the Deal)

It's funny how some stories become instantly memorable. During one of the breaks, I noticed two women sitting together, humming a tune. As a friendly human who appreciates music, I couldn't help but take notice.

When they saw that I was listening, they stopped and told me that we would win their business if I could guess the tune.

I'm pretty decent at music trivia and listen to many different genres of music. My specialty is 80s music, of course, since it's the best music! I knew the tune they were humming and told them I recognized it as "The Girl from Ipanema." They both went wide-eyed at this, and we all smiled and laughed.

We did indeed win the business, which was a $3.6 million opportunity for our company. I like to believe we won the business due to my careful preparation and approach to the presentation rather than based on answering the music question correctly.

Delivering a Demonstration in Clothes That Were Not Mine

The location for this meeting was a natural gas plant on the western coast of Australia near Karratha. Because this was an active plant, we were required to wear PPE (Personal Protective Equipment). They had requested our clothing and shoe sizes ahead of time so that the gear would be ready for us on the day of the meeting.

When we arrived, we were given our gear and provided access to the locker room to change and store our shoes, jackets, and any other items that we didn't need to carry into the plant. After changing, we all walked from the administrative building to the meeting and break room.

We start the meeting as described above with introductions and an overview before moving into my presentation of the solution. That all goes well, and after about six hours of meeting, we officially wrap up the meeting and spend some time casually chatting with the prospect's team.

We discussed the PPE, and I mentioned that this was the first time I'd ever presented while wearing it. They asked me if it created any challenges, and I shared that it was fine. Everything fit properly, but I kept getting a bit of a draft on the side of my legs.

Don't get ahead of me here!

After a beat, one of the "Ipanema" women from earlier asked if I had removed my pants when putting on the

PPE. I immediately started blushing, as that was precisely what I had done. To be fair, no one told me otherwise.

Everyone got a big laugh at my expense, but it was fine and didn't bother me. In fact, it helped to make the meeting memorable for everyone, and that's a perfect tease for the final chapter, **Chapter 8—Leave an Impression**.

Notes

Suggestions to Develop Your Storytelling Skill

You know the drill by now. Here are some suggestions for developing your storytelling ability. Don't overthink it. Telling stories is already part of your DNA. Practice, experiment, and find your storyteller's voice.

Practice Retelling Everyday Events

The best way to improve your storytelling is to practice telling stories. Make time with a colleague or family member and practice retelling the everyday events of your life.

Can you make that last trip to the grocery store interesting? If so, imagine how exciting your solution can be!

Did you crush that last run or workout? Tell someone about it as if it was an epic quest filled with peril at every turn. Enjoy the silly nature of it, and think about how you could inject some fun and levity into your next presentation.

Personalize a Customer Success Story

There are case studies and customer stories. The marketing team typically puts together case studies based on real-life customers, detailing the problem they wanted to solve and how they used your solution. These are usually published documents that you can share with prospects during the sales cycle.

Customer stories are less official. They are little anecdotes you can drop as proof points for your solution during your presentation. You want to use these to highlight a situation at a similar company to the one you're presenting to. In this instance, the details are not as important as the context.

I recommend you find one of those customer stories and learn it forward and backward. Again, don't sweat the details, but focus on their situation and how your solution solved it. Know the story well enough that it becomes one that you can share on the spot the next time the situation presents itself.

Book Recommendation:
Stories that Stick - by Kindra Hall

Kindra is a talented storyteller who engages you right from the beginning. You will read it faster than you expect because you become so invested in the stories she shares. This book is a must-read for improving your storytelling ability.

> "Memorable people do memorable things. Followers are seldom remembered. The herd mentality is the killer of innovation. When appropriate, be bold in your undertakings."
>
> – Gad Saad

Chapter 8 – Leave an Impression

We've arrived at the last Timeless Behavior, **"Leave an Impression."** When you create a memorable experience for your audience, they will be engaged, retain information from your presentation, and generally have a more positive experience. This can be a tremendous advantage when competing for attention and business in a crowded market.

What Does it Mean to be Memorable?

We all likely have examples of memorable people in our lives. It may be someone in your family or a teacher who connected with you early on. In our presales roles, we don't always have much time with our audiences, but when we do, we must consider ways to create that lasting impression.

Leave a Lasting Impression

Why should they remember you? Your goal in every presentation should be to be memorable. In a sea of similar products and solutions, standing out is essential. You want your audience to leave with a clear and positive recollection of you and your message. This can influence their decision-making process long after the presentation has ended. Here are some goals to keep in mind to create that lasting impression.

You were likable. Being personable and relatable goes a long way in making a lasting impression. Your presentation style has to showcase your own unique personality and charm. Do things that friendly humans do: make eye contact, smile, and laugh when appropriate. This likability factor often tips the scales in your favor when all other factors are equal.

You kept their interest. An engaging presentation holds the audience's attention from start to finish. You ensure that your audience remains captivated by storytelling, interactive elements, and dynamic delivery. When they are genuinely interested, they are more likely to remember the content. Interactive presentation tools such as MentiMeter allow your audience to respond to polls or questions through their phone. Interactivity can be a fantastic way to involve your audience in the presentation.

You kept the message simple. Complexity can be overwhelming and is quickly forgotten. Simplifying your message makes it more digestible and memorable. Clear, concise communication helps your audience grasp the core benefits of your solution without getting lost in technical details. Revisit some of the techniques from **Chapter 5 – Have a Conversation** about using simple language.

You made it look easy. Presenting with confidence and ease reassures your audience that your solution is effective and user-friendly. If you don't honestly believe in your solution, your audience will sense it. They will pick up on your energy. Demonstrating with competence and simplicity makes a strong impression, leaving your audience with a sense of assurance about their potential investment. The best way to increase your confidence and competence is through rehearsal and practice.

They could remember it (and share it). A memorable presentation can be easily recalled and shared with others. By structuring your content with a simple story, you empower your audience to advocate for your solution within their organization, amplifying your reach.

You made them feel something. Emotional connections are powerful and enduring. You create a lasting impact by evoking emotions through storytelling, empathy, and enthusiasm. When your audience feels something, whether it's excitement, relief, or inspiration, they are more likely to remember you and your message.

Connect With Your Audience on an Emotional Level

I cannot overstate the importance of emotionally connecting with your audience. Think back to the last movie that truly made you feel something. For me, it was Ghostbusters: Afterlife (2021). This film, directed by Jason

Reitman, the son of Ivan Reitman, who directed the original, was a loving continuation of the Ghostbusters movies from the 1980s. Jason's affection for the characters is evident throughout the film, and when familiar faces reappear on the screen, I tear up every time. While you may not be able to elicit such a dramatic response during your presentations, aiming for a similar level of engagement and connection is undoubtedly worthwhile.

Movies resonate because they tap into shared experiences and emotions. Similarly, when you present, consider what shared experiences you might have with your audience that you can weave into your story. This could be as straightforward as addressing a specific business problem that your platform solves.

Take, for example, an IT ticketing solution. Almost everyone who has worked with computers has faced issues requiring assistance from the IT team, typically managed through help desk tickets. By tapping into this common experience, you can connect with your audience on a personal level. You might share a story about when you struggled to get the IT help you needed, highlighting the frustrations of navigating a cumbersome ticketing system. Compelling storytelling in this context can evoke an emotional response from your audience as they recall similar experiences.

Bringing in shared experiences shows empathy and helps build trust. When your audience believes that you genuinely understand and want to help solve their problems, their skepticism diminishes, and their trust in you increases. This trust is crucial for establishing yourself as a trusted advisor.

In my experience, emotional connection is one of the most significant factors in winning large deals. When mentoring newcomers to the presales role, I emphasize the importance of being a friendly human, a concept I

Chapter 8 – Leave an Impression

also highlight on my LinkedIn profile. It underscores the value of creating emotional connections with your audience during presentations, a key strategy for gaining their trust and confidence.

Stand Apart from Other Presentations

In a competitive market, your presentation is just one of many that your audience will see. They are likely to sit through multiple demonstrations, each promising to solve their problems and meet their needs. This saturation of information can make it challenging for your presentation to stand out and leave a lasting impression.

As a result, many presentations start to blend together, looking and sounding the same. Companies will all have the "Nascar Slide" with the logos of the companies who have already chosen their solution. The pitch deck will likely point to an analyst report showing the solution in a favorable quadrant. This monotony can lead to disengagement and make it difficult for your audience to recall the specifics of any one presentation. The key to overcoming this is to find ways to differentiate yourself and your message from the rest.

So, what can you do to be different and memorable? Start with your content. Ensure your message is clear and compelling and directly addresses your audience's unique needs and pain points. Use case studies, anecdotes, and real-world examples to make your content relatable and tangible. The goal is to make your presentation informative but also relevant and engaging.

Delivery is equally essential. How you present your information can significantly impact its reception. Use storytelling techniques from **Chapter 7 – Tell a Story** to create a narrative flow. Engage your audience with dynamic body language, and vary your tone to maintain interest. Practice your delivery to be confident and fluid, ensuring you connect with your audience rather than just talking at them.

Finally, aim to create moments of surprise and delight. These can be small but impactful elements that capture attention and make your presentation memorable. For example, an unexpected but relevant analogy, a powerful visual, or an interactive element that involves the audience directly could be used. Such moments can break the monotony and leave a positive impression long after your presentation has ended.

By focusing on unique content, polished delivery, and creating moments of surprise and delight, you can ensure that your presentation stands out in the minds of your audience, making you memorable and setting you apart from the competition.

The Benefits of Being Memorable

If you aren't memorable, you are easily forgotten or simply blend into the background. To achieve real, lasting success in presales, you must be memorable and leave an impression on your audience. Here are some of the benefits I've experienced from being memorable.

Enhanced Brand - Personal and Company

Leaving a lasting impression through your presentations enhances your personal and the company's brand by raising awareness, creating positive associations, and fostering emotional connections. When your audience consistently experiences engaging and impactful presentations, they develop a favorable perception of you and your company, deepening trust and affinity.

This emotional resonance increases loyalty, making clients more likely to choose and advocate for your brand, thereby expanding your reputation and reach.

Better Networking and Relationships

Being memorable through your presentations enhances your networking and relationship-building efforts by fostering authentic connections and encouraging collaboration. This approach helps you develop a diverse network, opening up expanded growth opportunities and support from various contacts.

Increased Trust and Credibility

Leaving an impression in your presentations is crucial for building trust and credibility. You enhance your reputation and showcase your expertise by consistently delivering high-quality, transparent, and service-oriented presentations. This approach establishes you as a reliable and knowledgeable partner, strengthening your audience's trust in you and your solutions.

Differentiation in a Crowded Market

Being memorable in a crowded market ensures you stand out and draw attention to your solution. It means offering a unique experience for your audience that distinguishes your presentation from others. By demonstrating your expertise and a deep understanding of their needs, you create a lasting impression that differentiates you as a trusted and knowledgeable advisor in their eyes.

Four Techniques for Delivering a Memorable Presentation

I don't recall exactly when it happened, but it was very early in my presales career. I remember walking out of an on-site presentation where I did an excellent (technical) job showing our solution. I received praise from the seller and requisite the pat on the head, but as we were leaving the lobby, we noticed a team from our competitor getting ready to go in. Suddenly, it hit me that my audience was seeing other presentations, not just mine. I started thinking that those other presales folks probably did a good (technical) job showing their solution and believed they had also crushed it. They also probably got praise and a pat on the head.

I immediately started considering the presentation experience from the perspective of my audience. I imagined myself sitting through multiple presentations that began to look and sound the same. I thought about the things that would make one presentation stand out from the others and be memorable. I landed on four main points I focus on delivering whenever I present. I've shared these with mentees and people just starting their careers for many years. I'm going to include them here for you as well.

1. Be a Friendly Human

I've used the "friendly human" line for a while now, and while it seems completely obvious, I've seen very talented presales professionals come across as anything but friendly. They weren't unfriendly intentionally—they were simply focused on the wrong things.

With our engineer brains, we tend to focus too much on executing the task flawlessly. We spend time perfecting what we want to show the audience rather than considering what they need to see. We obsess over the clicks rather than the questions we should ask. In other words, our engineer tendencies take over, and we come across as something other than friendly—maybe more like nerdy or detached humans.

The good news is that your audience will see you as a friendly human if you truly practice the Timeless Behaviors. Here are some additional things that friendly humans do:

Friendly humans smile.
Having a friendly attitude during your presentations is crucial. Remember the "Most Respectful Interpretation" concept when receiving questions and feedback from your audience. Look for the positive and expect things to go well. If you look for the negative, you will likely find it. Remember the first behavior of being authentic. There's nothing worse than someone who is faking friendliness.

Friendly humans show interest in others.
Friendly humans are genuinely interested in other people and enjoy learning about them. It's incredible how often you can find random connections with people in your audience. It could be a shared interest in a sport or hobby, like tennis, or shared memories about a place you've both visited. These tidbits help nurture and build personal connections.

Friendly humans are curious.
Curiosity goes hand in hand with friendliness. Ask questions that show interest in understanding your audience's needs and perspectives. This

makes the interaction more engaging and helps tailor your presentation to be more relevant and impactful. It also shows that you care about them.

Friendly humans are kind.
Kindness costs nothing but can yield tremendous results. Simple acts of kindness, such as acknowledging someone's contribution or showing appreciation, can leave a lasting positive impression. Kindness is a universal language that resonates with everyone.

Friendly humans are helpful.
Always aim to be of service to your audience. Whether providing additional resources, offering to follow up with more detailed information, or simply ensuring their questions are thoroughly answered, being helpful demonstrates that you are committed to their success and satisfaction.

Thinking about these concepts during your presentations will make you more relatable and memorable and enhance your audience's overall experience. Being a friendly human is not about following a script but about genuinely connecting with people, understanding their needs, and showing that you care. This approach builds trust, fosters positive relationships, and ultimately leads to greater success in your presales efforts.

2. Tell a Story

No, you are not experiencing deja vu. There was indeed an entire chapter dedicated to the behavior of **Tell a Story**. In Chapter 7, we dove deep into the art of storytelling and its powerful impact on presentations. This section serves as a reminder that storytelling is a crucial technique for being memorable. Here's a quick refresher on key storytelling techniques to help you leave a lasting impression.

Have a narrative.
A well-structured narrative is the backbone of any memorable presentation. It provides a coherent flow that guides your audience through your message, making it easier for them to follow and understand. Begin with a compelling opening that grabs attention, build through a series of logical points, and conclude with a strong finish. This structure ensures your presentation is not just a series of disconnected points but a unified story that resonates with your audience.

Personalize it to your audience.
Tailoring your story to your audience's specific interests and needs makes it more relevant and engaging. Use examples, anecdotes, and scenarios that they can relate to. This personalization shows you understand their world and challenges, making your message more impactful. When your audience sees themselves in your story, they are more likely to remember it and, by extension, you.

Use plain language.
Clarity is critical in storytelling. Avoid jargon and complex terminology that can alienate or confuse your audience. Instead, use simple, straightforward language that everyone can understand. This approach ensures that your message is accessible and clear, making it easier for your audience to grasp and remember the key points. Plain language helps bridge the gap between you and your audience, building a stronger connection.

Take them on a journey.
A great story takes its audience on a journey with challenges, discoveries, and resolutions. This journey should mirror the transformation or impact your solution offers. By framing your presentation as a journey, you engage your audience's curiosity and emotions, keeping them invested in the outcome. This journey narrative helps your audience visualize the benefits and changes your solution can bring to their organization.

Have a happy ending.
Every great story deserves a satisfying conclusion. In your presentation, this means clearly illustrating the positive outcomes your audience can expect. Highlight success stories, potential benefits, and the resolution of their pain points. A happy ending leaves your audience with a positive impression, reinforcing the value of your solution and making your presentation more memorable.

By integrating these storytelling techniques into your presentations, you ensure that your message is heard and remembered. Storytelling transforms ordinary presentations into engaging and impactful experiences, making you and your message stand out in the minds of your audience.

3. Deliver Value

The third technique is about communicating the overall value or benefit your solution will provide. Your audience needs to see how your solution addresses their challenges and delivers tangible benefits. Here's how to effectively deliver value in your presentations:

Understand the challenge your audience wants to solve.
Start by thoroughly understanding your audience's primary challenges and pain points. This requires research and active listening to identify the

problems they are most concerned about. Demonstrating a deep understanding of their specific issues builds credibility and shows that your solution meets their needs. Knowing their challenges lets you align your presentation with their priorities, ensuring your message resonates with them.

Define the relative size of the problem.
Once you understand the challenges, it's important to define their relative size and impact. Use data, statistics, and real-world examples to quantify the issues. This helps your audience grasp the severity and urgency of their situation. By clearly defining the problem's magnitude, you set the stage for demonstrating the substantial value your solution can bring. This context makes it easier for your audience to appreciate the significance of your offering.

Dig into the pain.
Don't be afraid to delve into the specific pains associated with the problem. Describe the consequences and adverse outcomes that result from not addressing these issues. Highlight the inefficiencies, costs, and frustrations your audience experiences due to these unresolved challenges. By vividly illustrating the pain points, you create a sense of urgency and a compelling reason for your audience to seek a solution. This approach makes your presentation more relatable and impactful.

Illustrate the value of solving.
Clearly articulate the value of solving the identified problems. Explain how your solution can alleviate the pain and bring about positive change. Use concrete examples and case studies to show the potential improvements and benefits. This helps your audience envision your solution's direct impact on their organization. Highlight the immediate and long-term

value, emphasizing how your solution can drive efficiency, reduce costs, and enhance overall performance.

Highlight the benefits.
Finally, focus on the specific benefits your solution offers. Beyond just solving the problem, showcase your solution's additional advantages. These advantages could include increased productivity, better customer satisfaction, improved scalability, or enhanced competitive advantage. By highlighting the comprehensive benefits, you reinforce the overall value proposition of your solution. Connect these benefits directly to the challenges and pains you discussed, creating a cohesive and compelling narrative.

By following these steps, you can effectively communicate the value of your solution, making it clear why your audience should choose you over the competition. Delivering value is more than just presenting features; it's about showing how your solution can transform your audience's situation and drive meaningful results.

4. Stay at 30,000 Feet

Staying at a high level in your presentation ensures that your message remains clear and consumable. By keeping your presentation at 30,000 feet, you avoid overwhelming your audience with too many details while providing a comprehensive overview. This approach allows you to dive deeper into specific areas based on audience questions and interests as needed. Here's how to effectively maintain this balance:

KYSS – Keep Your Story Simple.
Simplicity is critical to a memorable and effective presentation. Keep your

story straightforward, focusing on the main points that resonate most with your audience. Avoid getting bogged down in complex technical details that detract from your core message. A simple, coherent story helps your audience understand and remember your key points, making it easier for them to connect with your solution. And regardless of what your marketing team says, no one cares or remembers your super-cool product names.

Dive down when needed to address questions.
While maintaining a high-level overview, be prepared to dive deeper into specific topics when your audience has questions. This flexibility demonstrates your expertise and ensures that you are addressing their concerns. Answering questions in depth when necessary shows that you are knowledgeable and responsive, which can build trust and credibility. However, always return to the high-level narrative to keep the presentation cohesive and on track.

Pull back on the stick.
Just as a pilot pulls back on the stick to ascend to a higher altitude, you should pull back to the high-level overview after addressing detailed questions. This helps to refocus the presentation on the broader narrative and prevents it from becoming too detailed or fragmented. By consistently returning to the big picture, you ensure your audience remains engaged and aligned with your overall message.

Consider retention and sharing.
Keeping your presentation at a high level aids in information retention and makes it easier for your audience to share your solution with others. When your audience is not overwhelmed with excessive details, they are more

likely to remember the key points of your presentation. Simple, high-level messages are more accessible to recall and can have a greater impact.

Additionally, a clear and concise presentation can be easily communicated to colleagues and decision-makers who were absent, extending the reach of your presentation and reinforcing your key points across a broader audience. By making it easy for others to understand and share your message, you increase the chances of your solution being advocated internally.

By staying at 30,000 feet and following these principles, you can create a compelling and memorable presentation that resonates with your audience and addresses their needs.

Delivering a memorable presentation involves more than just technical proficiency. It requires you to connect with your audience on a human level, tell compelling stories, communicate clear value, and maintain a high-level perspective that keeps your message clear and engaging. By being a friendly human, telling a story, delivering value, and staying at 30,000 feet, you can ensure that your presentations are impactful and memorable. These techniques help you stand out from the competition and leave a lasting impression on your audience, ultimately leading to greater success in your presales efforts.

Chapter 8 – Leave an Impression

Story Time: Krispy Kreme Donuts

One of my favorite account executives, Joe Bunner, got us a meeting with Krispy Kreme. Joe and I worked together like a Swiss watch—precise movements and everything perfectly coordinated. We had our discovery call and confirmed the business challenges they were looking to solve. Our solution matched the requirements, and we clearly understood the benefits they could receive from implementing our platform.

Due to scheduling issues, I could not join Joe on-site for the meeting. He would be in person at the Krispy Kreme office, and I would support the presentation remotely from my home office.

If you don't mind a little side story here, while I prefer being in person—I'm a friendly human, after all—I don't mind virtual meetings when they make sense. I did my first virtual meeting in 1999, shortly after I began my presales career. We were using this new tool called WebEx. You can Google this if you don't believe me, but WebEx (this is pre-Cisco) had an advertising campaign at the time starring RuPaul. The commercial is on YouTube and has RuPaul wearing a dress in the WebEx colors of blue and green. The tagline at the end of the commercial is "We've got to start meeting like this!" So, yes, I've been doing virtual meetings for a while.

A Friendly Human in Presales

Getting back to our Krispy Kreme story, knowing I would be virtual, I quickly hatched a plan and shared it with Joe. The morning of our demo, I ran by my local Krispy Kreme and grabbed a dozen hot, fresh donuts and one of their iconic hats.

Back at my desk, I positioned the donuts perfectly so they were captured in view of my camera. I put on my hat and was ready to go. Quality control is always important, so I decided to have a taste test, leaving the box with one donut missing.

The time came to start the meeting. I joined with my camera off while Joe provided notes from our previous meetings and set the context for the day. He wrapped up, and it was time for me to start showing their solution. I turned my camera on, and they saw me in the hat with their product prominently displayed behind me.

Now, imagine if I had done the typical prep—reviewed the standard slides, double-checked the technical details, and rehearsed the demo flow. Sure, it would have been professional and technically sound, but it would have been just another virtual meeting. It would have blended into the sea of meetings and vendor pitches they receive every week.

What happened next was something special. As I started the presentation, I could see smiles and nods all around. The reaction was immediate—they all engaged right away and felt "in" on the story. There's something about seeing your product in action, even in a playful context, that gets people excited. It wasn't just a presentation anymore—it was an experience. I could see the rapport building in real-time, and that subtle connection we made with their brand gave us an edge, beyond just the technicalities of the solution.

The solution presentation went well due to our careful attention to their needs, and we received very positive feedback after the meeting. The best feedback was landing a significant deal with them shortly afterward. While we can't attribute the win entirely to the hat and donuts, we can't not attribute it to them either.

Not every meeting will provide this type of branding opportunity, but what's interesting is that this kind of personal touch often outlives the actual business transaction. A few years after the Krispy Kreme deal, I ran into someone at a tradeshow who had been in that meeting. They didn't mention the technical aspects of our solution. Instead, they brought up the demo—the hat, the donuts, and how memorable the entire experience was. While people may forget the specs of your solution, they won't forget how you made them feel during the process. The hat and donuts weren't just a gimmick—they were thoughtfully tied to Krispy Kreme's brand, showing we understood their identity and creating a genuine connection. That's what made the story stick with them long after the deal was done, proving that sometimes the smallest personal touches can make the biggest impact and that's the power of leaving an impression.

Notes

Suggestions to Develop Being Memorable

As with the other timeless behaviors, I am leaving you with some thoughts on how to develop being memorable. Some technical people find this challenging as they don't enjoy having the focus placed squarely on them. With intention and practice, I believe you can build this into a comfortable, reliable skill that will drive success in your career.

Develop Visual Aids that are Different and Unique

Do you remember the clip art from the 1990s? Man, was it bad. What's worse, some companies are still using it.

Try to find unique and interesting images to help convey concepts in your presentation. No one likes to read text on a slide; the only thing worse is for you to read it to them verbatim.

Here's a quick example. Let's assume you have a slide that details the potential benefits your audience will receive from implementing your solution. Those benefits include reduced labor expenses, time savings through increased efficiency, and higher sales due to more time to work opportunities.

Instead of writing all that out, consider having only three images on the slide;
- Icon for Money (a bill or coins) to represent reduced labor cost
- Clock Icon to represent time savings
- Chart Icon with a line going up to represent higher sales

Your audience is more likely to remember three images than all those words.

Seek Feedback on Memorable Moments

When you have those "aha" moments in a presentation, take the time to ask your audience why they had the reaction they had. Consider doing this as the meeting is wrapping up. Asking the question could sound something like this:

"Would you mind if I asked you all a question? There was a definite reaction in the room earlier when I showed you the gizmo function. Could you share why you found that so interesting, surprising, or valuable?"

The goal is to understand why the moment was memorable and use that feedback to create more of those moments in the future.

Reflect on and Develop Your Personal Brand

Your brand is the unique combination of skills, experiences, and personality you bring to your professional interactions. It's what sets you apart from others and leaves a lasting impression on your audience. To begin this process, reflect on your core values, strengths, and areas of expertise. Consider what makes you unique and how you want to be perceived by others.

Ask yourself questions like:
- What are my most significant achievements?
- What feedback do I consistently receive from colleagues and clients?
- What am I passionate about in my work?

This self-reflection will help you identify the key elements that define your personal brand. Once you clearly understand your personal brand, focus on developing and communicating it effectively.

Continually Practice and Develop the Seven Timeless Behaviors

Many perceive self-improvement as a linear progression—a step-by-step journey from one level to the next, guided by insights gained from books, gurus, or seminars. However, true growth and lasting change require more than just absorbing information; they demand an ongoing commitment to learning, applying, and refining new behaviors and skills. It's not enough to read a book recommended by a colleague; the real value comes from actively integrating its teachings into daily practice.

Personal growth is a continual cycle of learning, application, and refinement. It involves consistently reflecting on one's actions, identifying areas for improvement, and actively working to develop and practice new behaviors. This iterative process allows individuals to internalize new knowledge, adapt it to their unique circumstances, and refine their approaches over time. Without this active engagement, the potential benefits of any self-improvement resource—whether a book, a course, or a mentor's advice—remain largely untapped.

Therefore, the key to meaningful self-improvement lies in acquiring knowledge and the deliberate and sustained effort to apply and refine that knowledge. By embracing this cycle of learning and practice, individuals can truly transform their professional abilities and drive personal growth.

I hope you have enjoyed this book and the stories contained within. More importantly, I hope you recognize the transformative potential within the Seven Timeless Behaviors: **Be Authentic, Listen Actively, Show Empathy, Have a Conversation, Practice Humility, Tell a Story**, and **Leave an Impression.** Implementing these behaviors can elevate your performance and achievements in presales.

I encourage you to allocate dedicated time regularly for self-reflection on these behaviors, assess your application of them, and continually refine your approach. This intentional practice will solidify your grasp of these principles and propel your growth and success.

The Seven Timeless Behaviors

1. **Be Authentic**
   Showcase your values, unique charm and personality.

2. **Listen Actively**
   Listen to understand rather than to respond.

3. **Show Empathy**
   Consider the perspective of others.

4. **Have a Conversation**
   Keep the communication flowing two ways, not just one.

5. **Practice Humility**
   It's not about you. It's about others.

6. **Tell a Story**
   Engage and connect through compelling narratives.

7. **Leave an Impression**
   Deliver an experience your audience will not forget.

Notes

References

Angelou, M. (n.d.). People may forget what you say. People may forget what you do. But people will never forget how you make them feel. [Source Unknown].

Brown, B. (2007, February). I Thought It Was Just Me (but it isn't): Making the Journey from "What Will People Think?" to "I Am Enough". Avery.

Brown, B. (2010, June). The power of vulnerability [Video]. TED Conferences. https://www.ted.com/talks/brene_brown_the_power_of_vulnerability

Brown, B. (2012, September). Daring Greatly: How the Courage to Be Vulnerable Transforms the Way We Live, Love, Parent, and Lead. Avery.

Capote, T. (1980). Too Brief a Treat: The Letters of Truman Capote. New York, NY: Random House.

Care, J. (2002). Mastering Technical Sales: The Sales Engineer's Handbook. (1st ed.) Artech House

Celebrity Net Worth. (2024). Tom Hanks Net Worth. Retrieved from https://www.celebritynetworth.com/richest-celebrities/actors/tom-hanks-net-worth/

Cohan, P. (2003). Great Demo! How To Create And Execute Stunning Software Demonstrations. iUniverse.

Davis, M. (1980). It's Hard to be Humble. On Hard to Be Humble [Album]. Casablanca Records.

Epictetus. (n.d.). We have two ears and one mouth, so we can listen twice as much as we speak. Retrieved from Goodreads.com.

Falcone, R. (2014). Just F*ing Demo: : Tactics for Leading Kickass Product Demos. CreateSpace Independent Publishing Platform

Forbes, M. (n.d.). The art of conversation lies in listening. Retrieved from Goodreads.com.

Ford, H. (n.d.). If there is any one secret of success, it lies in the ability to get the other person's point of view and see things from his angle as well as your own. Retrieved from Goodreads.com.

Gottschall, J. (2012). The Storytelling Animal: How Stories Make us Human. Boston, MA: Mariner Books.

Hall, K. (2019). Stories That Stick: How Storytelling Can Captivate Customers, Influence Audiences, and Transform Your Business. HarperCollins Leadership.

Jobs, S. (2005, June 12). Stanford commencement address. Stanford University. Retrieved from https://news.stanford.edu/2005/06/12/jobs-061505/

Lathrap, M. T. (1895). Judge softly. Retrieved from https://jamesmilson.com/about-the-blog/judge-softly-or-walk-a-mile-in-his-moccasins-by-mary-t-lathrap/

Merriam-Webster. (n.d.). Authentic. In Merriam-Webster.com dictionary. Retrieved April, 2024, from https://www.merriam-webster.com/dictionary/authentic

Perry, K. E. G. (2022, June 23). Tom Hanks says it's an 'honour' to crash weddings, after being repeatedly photographed with newly-wed couples. The Independent. https://www.independent.co.uk

Richo, D. (2008). The Five Things We Cannot Change: And The Happiness We Find by Embracing Them. Boston, MA: Shambhala Publications. Retrieved from Goodreads.com.

Saad, G. (n.d.). Memorable people do memorable things. Followers are seldom remembered. The herd mentality is the killer of innovation. When appropriate, be bold in your undertakings. Retrieved from https://www.goodreads.com/author/quotes/29563.Gad_Saad

Sorenson, M. (2017). I Hear You: The Surprisingly Simple Skill Behind Extraordinary Relationships. Autumn Creek Press.

Thesaurus.com. (2020, December). When was writing invented? Thesaurus.com. Retrieved from https://www.thesaurus.com/e/writing/when-was-writing-invented/

White, C. (2019). The Six Habits of Highly Effective Sales Engineers. DemoDoctor.com

Wikipedia contributors. (2023, July 16). The Tortoise and the Hare. In Wikipedia, The Free Encyclopedia. Retrieved from https://en.wikipedia.org/wiki/The_Tortoise_and_the_Hare

Wilde, O. (n.d.). Be yourself; everyone else is already taken. [Source Unknown].

Words Alive. (2018, September 5). The history of storytelling. Retrieved from https://www.wordsalive.org/blog/2018/9/5/the-history-of-storytelling

www.ingramcontent.com/pod-product-compliance
Lightning Source LLC
Chambersburg PA
CBHW071827210526
45479CB00001B/31